THREE STRONG WESTERN WOMEN

THREE STRONG WESTERN WOMEN

A Play by Carol Sletten

With Background Material
by Eric Kramer

Illustrated by Carol Sletten

Wolf Water Press

www.WolfWaterPress.com

PO Box 588, Pinetop, AZ 85935

Library of Congress Control Number: 2013936626

Publisher's Cataloging-in-Publication

Sletten, Carol.
    Three strong western women : a play / by Carol
    Sletten ; with background material by Eric Kramer ;
    illustrated by Carol Sletten. — 1st ed.
        p. cm.
    Includes bibliographical references and index.
    LCCN 2013936626
    ISBN 978-0-9892024-0-4

    1. Women—West (U.S.)—Biography—Drama. 2.
Women—
    West (U.S.)—History—Drama. 3. Mormons—West (U.S.)—
    Biography—Drama. 4. Women missionaries—West (U.S.)—
    Biography—Drama. 5. Apache women—West (U.S.)—
    Biography—Drama. 6. Frontier and pioneer life—Drama.
    7. West (U.S.)—Biography—Drama. I. Kramer, Eric,
    1951- II. Title.

PS3619.L47S54 2013   812'.6
                    QBI13-600058

First Edition

Second Printing

Manufactured in the United States of America

Carol Sletten
Copyright 2012

Lozen -- *Apache warrior woman*

Emma Lee -- *Mormon handcart pioneer*

Minnie Guenther -- *Missionary to the Apaches*

Dedication

This book is dedicated to our daughters,
Sibyl Heather and Selena Kirsten,
and to all strong Western women
of the past, present and future.

Contents

Illustrations

Introduction

The idea to write *Three Strong Western Women* came to me in a flash. I knew instantly what the title would be, which women I'd be writing about and that they needed to tell their own stories if I wanted them to be able to reach across time and connect with people living today.

When artists and writers decide to be honest, we admit that magical flashes of insight usually come to us only after we've done a lot of preliminary work. In this case I'd spent many years researching and illustrating Western subjects as well as co-authoring *Story of the American West: Legends of Arizona*.

Though my admiration for Emma, Minnie and Lozen began when my husband, Eric Kramer, and I were writing that history, it was an invitation to speak at a luncheon called "Wine, Women and Wow" that sparked my imagination and made me decide to drop everything and write about them.

Deciding to do the play was fast and fun. The hard part was figuring out how to tell each of the character's complicated stories in less than 20 minutes while helping the audience see them as unique individuals. So I set out to find everything I could about their lives and times before I took each magnificent woman, separately, into my mind for about a month while I wrote her story.

I relied heavily on historical sources written from the point of view of each woman's culture and belief system to help me imagine what and how she would tell me about her life and circumstances. The works of Juanita Brooks, a well-regarded Mormon historian, helped me understand Emma Lee. When it was time to write about Minnie Guenther, I was lucky enough to find a recording of her own voice to guide me through her life. She had a delightful chuckle. There are, of course, no recordings of Lozen so I read and reread the words of an old

1

Apache who had been on the warpath with the warrior woman when he was a boy. His stories, recorded in a book by the historian Eve Ball, introduced me to the Gray Ghost, the two beautiful women, the 12 warriors and Lozen's horse power. Those and other details from the oral history helped me look at Lozen though the eyes of her own people.

The play has a life of its own. More performances are being scheduled. But because people have been so intrigued by the women's stories and want to know more, we decided to publish the play along with historical background material.

There are two very different styles of writing in this book. The play is a work of creative non-fiction, while the history chapters are clear and crisp explanations of the issues and events that surrounded the women during their lives. Eric, who has a strong and distinguished background in journalism, wrote those chapters.

Act One

Emma Lee
1836 – 1897

Home….home…that simple little word holds a deep meaning for most of us womenfolk. It is especially poignant to a pioneer woman like me.

I remember whispering "home" over and over again while I was pushing or pulling a heavy handcart across the desert and through the mountains. I wasn't homesick for the dreary, impoverished town that I had left behind in England. I was dreaming about my future in the golden West – the future promised to me by the Mormon missionaries. The idea of having a home in Zion helped me endure my hunger and thirst, the unbearably hot and cold weather, and most of all – the look of suffering in the eyes of my sick and dying companions. At times the murmured sound brought forth a faint image of heaven, which helped me bear the bitter sorrow of having to leave so many of my fellow converts in shallow graves along the trail.

I think God let me hang on to the word "Home"

because He understood I was too tired and discouraged to string together enough words to form a prayer. He knew I needed extra strength so that I could take care of all the immigrants who were falling ill along the trail. And He gave it to me. How else could I have pushed a malnourished mother and her newborn in a handcart for two days after I had exhausted myself helping them both survive the birth?

The word "home" was on my mind in a bittersweet way when I hobbled into Salt Lake City in the company of my half-starved, frostbitten brothers and sisters. We were certainly a sadly diminished remnant of our original party of newly converted Latter-day Saints, who had left Iowa City with so much optimism.

After thanking God for helping me survive the tribulations of our 1,300-mile trek, I fell to my knees and told Him that if He'd give me a family, I'd do everything in my power to make them feel like they had a real home no matter how difficult the circumstances or how desolate the location.

Today, 40 years after I made that promise, my family's home is in Winslow, Arizona, a dusty little railroad town where folks call me Doctor Grandma French.

Of course, I wouldn't be recognized by that name in the wider world. Most people think of me as Emma Lee, the 17th plural wife of John D. Lee, the only man to be convicted and executed for the 1857 Mountain Meadows Massacre.

Well, since I brought it up, I'd better tell you about that horrible tragedy before you hear the rest of my story. I can't give you a first-hand account because the massacre happened three months before I met the magnificent man, who would become my husband.

And as strange as it seems, I didn't hear about the massacre until the spring of 1859, almost a year and a half after my marriage. Nobody had discussed it in my presence in Salt Lake City where I had been working as an indentured servant, nor did I hear anyone mention it after John took me to live with his other wives and children in Harmony.

Looking back, I realize the family must have been talking about the massacre when they excluded me from so many of their stern-faced conversations. John had probably told them not to talk about it in front of me because he didn't think I was ready to know about such a horrible thing happening less than an hour's horseback ride from my new home.

But during those early months of my marriage, I thought I was being excluded from family pow-wows because John's other wives didn't like sharing him with a new bride.

I certainly had to struggle against jealousy and resentment when John took two more wives after he married me. I don't suppose any of you ladies have ever had to share your husband with other wives – or if you have, your husband probably didn't have as many other wives as John did.

Even so, I'm sure you'll understand why it was hard for me to remain cheerful. How would you feel if you had to work ceaselessly taking care of your husband's big family and building up the value of his property when you might not see him for days or weeks on end because he had other wives and children who needed him elsewhere?

Sometimes, I'd have a good cry. Other times, I'd think about the first time I saw John preaching in the church – the way his eyes pierced into mine and claimed me with a holy force... And I'd remember how wonderful it felt to be noticed by such a handsome, distinguished and successful member of Brigham Young's inner-circle. If those memories weren't enough, I'd give myself a good hard scolding. I'd remind myself that I had been sealed to John in the temple ONLY after being fully informed that my future husband had been chosen by the church's leaders to follow the sacred principle of marrying more than one wife.

Though my dissatisfaction never completely disappeared, I felt more confident after I resolved to keep a special place in my husband's heart by putting his welfare above all others. That was my personal principle. And I held to that promise until my beloved was executed by a firing squad in 1877.

I bore his children, nursed his family, cooked, cleaned, sewed, gardened, scrubbed clothes and ran his boarding house. I even did heavy work on his farm and places of business of the kind that is usually reserved for men. As time went on, I formed a strong bond with most of John's other wives and their children – especially the wee ones. I was always the one selected to plan and cook meals for Brigham Young and other important church leaders who used to come to Harmony to confer with our husband. Though John may have valued me mostly for my culinary and business skills, I felt closest to God when I was caring for the sick or helping one of my sister-wives bring a new child into the world.

I was heavy with my own first child when John's oldest wife led me into the orchard to tell me about the Mountain Meadows Massacre. She said it was about time that I knew what happened not long before I married John – how some Indians had slaughtered a wagon train of gentiles in a nearby mountain pass. When I looked alarmed, she patted me on the belly and said I needn't worry because Indians liked and respected our husband. "No" she continued, "our family doesn't have to worry about Indians. But we do have enemies – and those vicious people have told the government that John ordered the massacre. That's why he needs to get away before the soldiers come to arrest him. We've been warned that they're on their way and will be here tomorrow."

I was too confused and distressed to ask questions so I followed her inside and helped the others bundle up provisions for John to take to his hideout.

When the soldiers arrived about noon the next day, the commanding officer didn't seem surprised to find John absent. The captain just shook his head and asked the three of us who were outside if we knew why the army wanted to arrest our husband. When we didn't answer, he said, "John D. Lee is a murderer." He went on to tell us that John's Mormon Militia and Indian allies had slaughtered over 120 unarmed men, women and children. He said they had killed almost everyone in a wagon train that was passing through southern Utah on the way to California. He asked us if we were proud of the way John had participated in the bloodbath at Mountain Meadows, and of the way the head of our household and his cohorts had slaughtered everyone except the tiniest of their children. "If you are," he shouted, "you should also be proud of how your esteemed husband and his fellow 'saints' picked through those bodies for valuables before they rounded up the poor souls' cattle and horses to enrich their own herds."

That was it. I couldn't listen to any more of the government man's hateful lies. I turned and made my way down to the creek as fast as my pregnant belly would allow. When I got there, I bent over and splashed water on my face over and over again. I wanted the water to wash away the memory of what I had just heard. But it didn't. My distress turned into dizziness, which made me fall on a jagged rock and bruise my unborn baby.

John came back and comforted me after I gave birth to a stillborn son a month later. And because the Civil War took the military away from Utah, he was able to continue his life as a Mormon patriarch for quite a few years after that. During the next decade, he took two more wives, bought more property, built more houses for his wives, expanded his farm and businesses, and continued to father children, six of them with me.

We had some happy times during those years even though we knew that more and more people were blaming John for the massacre. By 1870, the church leaders had even turned against him.

There are many things that I'll never understand about John. One of them is why he followed Brigham Young's orders to sell everything at Harmony and move some of his families into remote locations even after Young had excommunicated him.

That's how I ended up running the famous ferry that helped so many Mormon pioneers cross the Colorado River so they could settle in Arizona. My oldest son and I would load the wooden boat, one wagon and team per trip, and struggle to get it across the wide river. Travelers paid us three dollars for each wagon and 75 cents for each horse. My children and I lived in Lonely Dell and operated Lee's Ferry from 1872 to 1879. We ran the ferry before John was arrested, while he was in jail, during his two trials and for two years after he was executed.

We loved our home at Lonely Dell and even though it was a challenge to keep Lee's Ferry running through all the equipment breakdowns, floods, rockslides and threats of Indian attacks, I resented it when the Mormons ordered my family to leave. And I was devastated when their agent gave us only 14 of the 100 head of cattle that they had promised to pay us for the ferry.

The silver lining to my family's situation came in the form of Frank French, a prospector who helped us move farther into Arizona and start over again. Though Frank is not a great man like John was, he is an honorable and honest man. And he helped us when no one else would. Since Frank and I got along so well on the trail, we decided to get married when we got to Snowflake.

I can only describe our early days in Arizona as hardscrabble. We moved five times before we finally settled here in Winslow. I've become the family's breadwinner since Frank goes off to prospect for many months at a time. But having to support a family is nothing new to me. I was my family's main breadwinner for many years when I was married to John.

My problem was that I didn't know how to create a happy home in a place where my children were being insulted and shunned. It was hard for them to hear people calling their father a vicious murderer. I've lived though many sorrowful events in my life but none of them hurt me as much as learning that my beautiful sixteen-year-old daughter had killed herself because she thought other young people were blaming her for the Mountain Meadows Massacre.

After Vickie died, I forced myself to go on living for the sake of my other children and for all the people who needed my doctoring. But some of my ideas changed. Until then, I'd always believed that my strength came from God. I still do – though I now know that most of it flows into me from the needs of others. That's the reason I'm content to live in Winslow. The railway workers, Indians, expectant mothers, Chinamen, Mexicans, cowhands and shady ladies that I doctor aren't exactly the saints that I expected to have as neighbors when I was longing to live in Zion. But I love each and every one of them and I know that God does too.

Act Two

Minnie Guenther
1890- 1982

Never in my wildest dreams did I think I'd be Mother of the Year for the entire country. But look – here it is – the certificate that names me 1967 National Mother of the Year.

What a surprise that something like that could happen to me! I can't even remember the last time that I dreamed about anything for myself – partly because my life has been so rich and fulfilling – but mostly because I've lived for 56 years among the Apaches, whose needs are so much greater than mine.

I did, of course, have many fanciful dreams when I was little. Some of them were pretty silly and fell out of my mind fairly soon. But my two favorites stayed with me – my dream of becoming a mother and the dream I had of becoming a missionary. And do you know that God in his goodness fulfilled both of those dreams? He gave me nine wonderful children and allowed me to become a helpmate to a loving and dedicated missionary.

But I wasn't thinking about those dreams while I was getting ready to attend our church's Thanksgiving service when I was 20 years old. I was trying not to think about a certain tall, very shy, seminary student who had turned down my family's invitation to come to Thanksgiving dinner. After I took a little time to tidy my hair and twist my mouth into a smile, I darted out the door and ran right smack into the very man I had been trying to forget.

I was not only surprised. I was annoyed! "What are you doing here, Edgar Guenther?" I asked. "You said you weren't coming. You told me you had too much work to do."

Edgar blinked a few times and got right to the point. "I just accepted a call to go to Arizona to the Apache Indians and want to know if you'll come along."

"Oh?... ahhh.......Oh! ...ummm...Yes, sure I'll go along," I said, as I grabbed his hand and pulled him down the walkway. "But right now I have to get to the church. I'm supposed to sing a solo this morning. Hurry."

Well, that was just the beginning of a whole lot of hurrying because the Wisconsin Synod

Lutheran Missionary Board wanted us to leave in two weeks. We weren't able to leave that quickly, but we did head out for Arizona almost right after our wedding on December 28th, 1910.

Goodness gracious, just getting to that remote reservation was a big challenge.

Arizona, especially the reservation, was entirely different from my home in Wisconsin and Edgar's home in South Dakota. The area was still a wilderness. The first thing we noticed were the mountains. Some were forested and snow-covered. Others were dark and craggy – or streaked in the colors of a rainbow. And the roads, oh my, they were really only muddy, rocky, rutty trails, with no bridges to help travelers cross the canyons, streams and rivers.

But the biggest difference was in the way the Apaches lived. They didn't live in houses. They lived in rounded, brush-covered tepees called wickiups. Women did all the heavy work. They carried water in pitch-covered baskets strapped to bands on their heads. They tanned hides, gathered firewood and grew corn and other crops in small plots. The women wore colorful, two-piece, full-skirted camp dresses made of calico. Though some Apache men dressed like cowboys, many still wore breechcloths and leggings and tall moccasins with turned up toes.

Children, who had been forced to go away to government schools, and then sent back after they got TB or eye diseases, were almost the only ones who could speak to us in English.

The Indians held their medicine men and ceremonies in very high regard. During the early years of our mission, we thought it was our duty to discourage the Apaches from attending those unchristian ceremonies. But now that I look back, I realize that those ceremonies and traditional customs helped the Indians live proper and respectful lives. Before the government forced the Apaches to live like white men, the reservation didn't have all the violence, alcoholism and divorce like it does now.

The Indians didn't seem to be the least bit wild and dangerous even though the Apache wars had ended only 25 years before we settled into our little house in East Fork. They loved to laugh and were very friendly to us. Edgar and I felt like we could've helped even the most traditionally minded Apaches come to Christ — if they hadn't had to struggle to survive amidst conditions of unrelenting poverty and disease.

So in addition to preaching the Gospel – building a school, orphanage, and several churches – Edgar and I thought it was our Christian duty to bring food, medicine and blankets to the sick and dying Apaches.

They really appreciated our visits. In fact, we were able to perform our first baptism because a little boy's heart was opened by one of those simple acts of kindness.

It happened after I told a child stricken with TB that I couldn't bring him food as often as I wished because it took me such a long time to walk the seven miles to his family's remote camp. You see, in those early days, Edgar and I didn't have any form of transportation other than our legs. We didn't even have horses.

Well, the consumptive boy and his family laughed and teased me about being too skinny to walk that far. After that, the boy became quite a friend of mine. He looked forward to having us read him Bible stories.

But one day he interrupted my husband's story with a loud whisper. He said, "I not be here long. Baptize me quick."

When Edgar agreed and turned to explain the ceremony to several adults who were sitting by the fire – just waiting for the child to die – the boy called out, "Come here. Baptize me now. You can talk to them anytime after I am gone."

That was more than 50 years ago, and yet I have a clear memory of how peaceful that sweet child's face looked after his baptism, and how grateful I was to God for sending us to his camp on that particular day – because, you see, the boy died before we could get back to see him again.

A reporter called me today because of the Mother of the Year Award. He wanted me to tell him what it was like to give birth without the help of doctors, and how I managed to take care of my big family in such a remote location and still find time to help my husband with his work at the school, church and orphanage.

Most of all, he was interested in how I nursed the Apaches during the 1918 great flu epidemic – how I rode into their remote camps with a can of milk hanging on one side my horse and a can of soup hanging on the other side.

Well, I've done a little writing myself. I wrote articles for missionary societies and pamphlets for Sunday school classes as well as helping my husband with his sermons. I knew what the fellow was up to. He wanted to slant the story to make it look like I'd had a miserable life instead of telling people about my many blessings.

So I told him that he should be writing about how hard it had been for the Apaches during our years on the reservation. Here's what I told him.

The reservation had constant plagues of smallpox, scarlet fever, diphtheria, whooping cough, typhoid fever, cholera, pneumonia, measles and most of all – eye diseases and TB. We were told that half of the Apache population had TB when we arrived on the reservation in 1911.

Death seemed to be everywhere. We'd often hear the eerie sound of Apache women keening and wailing after their loved ones had died. Even if we weren't close enough to hear them crying, we'd know that someone had died when we rode into their camps because they'd chop off their hair when they were in mourning.

Those diseases were even more devastating because the people were so terribly poor. And I want you to know that their poverty came about from their limited circumstances, not because they were lazy! Our Apaches worked hard! They farmed small plots of land, raised cattle and made beautiful handcrafts – which I often helped them sell to the outside world. But that brought in only a meager income for some of our Apaches. Many others had to leave the reservation to find work, for which they were paid only a fraction of what the white workers earned. There were natural disasters too – droughts, floods, and even an earthquake.

The combination of all those tribulations caused a great number of Apaches to doubt – not only our Christian teachings – but also their own traditional beliefs. Many became susceptible to the unhealthy claims of religious cults, which sprout up whenever people lose all hope of ever being able to live better lives. My husband was heartbroken when two of those cults claimed the hearts of hundreds our own White Mountain Apaches – especially since both used Christian symbols in their ceremonies.

Though God didn't always answer our prayers when we asked Him to help our Apache friends, He did give us many blessings. He gave us nine wonderful children, who warmed our hearts no matter what was happening outside the circle of our own loving family. And God never let my husband and me get discouraged at the same time!

Edgar died six years ago. And even though I have a big loving family and many dear Apache friends, I miss him sometimes like a stab in the heart. I wish he could be here to tell you about our missionary work. Edgar had such a wonderful way with words. The Apaches loved to hear him preach in their own language – which we both learned to speak fairly quickly. They appreciated how he helped them with practical things. But most of all, I think they respected him for his sincere honesty.

In fact, the Apaches respected my husband so much that they'd usually come to me when they were puzzled about religious matters. You see, they didn't want to upset their tall missionary friend by questioning his unwavering faith.

If you know anything about Apaches, you probably know that they don't usually come right out and ask you delicate questions. They used to say things like, "I heard a woman wondering about something… That woman doesn't understand why God wants the tall missionary to put water on our heads so we can go to heaven. I guess that woman was thinking about her dead relatives, how God won't let them into his happy place because they aren't baptized. That woman doesn't understand why Christians say God loves everyone when he is mean to Apaches who aren't baptized."

Oh, my! ....Questions like that were hard for me to answer because they echoed some of my own uncertainties. So I learned to answer them indirectly. I'd say, "I don't think anyone would know how to answer that woman's questions, because nobody has God's great wisdom. But if that woman came to me, I'd tell her that God is love, and since God is love, we can trust Him to be merciful." Then I'd sing, "Jesus loves me this I know for the Bible tells me so."

I have to admit that after all my years of missionary work, I don't know anything more about religion than I did before I left my safe and orderly Midwestern life to come and live with Edgar here on the reservation.

God is the only one who knows if we saved many souls.

What I do know is that Edgar and I saved many Apaches lives, and that we came to love the Apache people unconditionally!

Act Three

Approximately - 1840-1890

The moon is hanging low in the sky. He's watching me roam around like a ghost, while memories of battles, lost and won, haunt my mind and make me weary.

I'm too restless to sleep since I know nothing will be the same after we surrender tomorrow.

We will be taken to a place called Florida – a place so far away in the direction of the rising sun that we will never be able to escape and come home again.

Never again will we be able to find refuge in the cliffs and canyons that we know so well.

Never again will we be able to sense the Creator's presence on the summits of our sacred peaks, or feel His healing Power in the water of our Sacred Springs.

We are the last of our people to be free. After we surrender, the Earth will never again hear the sound of FREE Apaches laughing with our children, or hear the hooves of our horses thundering over the land of our ancestors.

After tonight, I will be a diminished person –
only HALF of what I have been. I will never again
wear the garment of a Two-Sided Woman.

I will take off this medicine robe and bury it
deep inside a cave. And then, when I see the first
faint glow of daylight creeping up over the mountains, I will tear my spirit in two and leave the
warrior side of myself next to the cave.

Ussen created me to be a Two-Sided Woman.

I didn't know that when I was a child living in
the land of my people near our sacred Warm
Springs.

I was busy learning how to use a knife, ride
horses, shoot, and run like the wind before I disappeared into thin air.

Apaches are born into a wild and beautiful
world – a world that is both dangerous and wonderful. We have many enemies so we train all our
children to be tough.

I was the toughest and fastest child that anyone had ever seen. Nobody could keep up with
me!

My victories made the women in my clan laugh
and shout and stomp their feet. Nana, our old

war chief, would laugh with them. He'd hold up his hands and howl like a coyote whenever he'd see me outrun, outshoot and outride the boys.

My older brother, Victorio, was proud of me, too. He let me come along when he and his friends were tracking game, rounding up wild horses and practicing to be warriors.

I liked keeping up with those much older, long-legged youths. It was worth it to put up with their teasing because they turned me into a ferocious fighter!

Nana had a talk with me after Victorio became a famous warrior. He told me I would be allowed to ride with my brother when I got older IF I knew how to heal wounds.

That idea pleased me very much until I realized I'd have to talk to our medicine woman. Nana saw the sour look on my face and asked me what was wrong.

I told him our healer would NOT want to be my teacher because she considered me to be a wild and willful child. The old warrior laughed. He said, "Tache's right. You are willful. Use that strong will of yours to turn her mind around."

Tache did become my teacher, but not because of anything I did. She decided to let me follow her around and do ALL her heavy work after she dreamed about me riding on a rainbow… That's what she said…

Nana liked to tease me about that. He said Tache had dreamed about how nice it would be to have a strong child chop all her wood and haul all her water.

I was too busy learning how to heal with plants and what to do when babies are ready to come into the world to pay any attention to his silly words. Tache was my teacher until the Gray Ghost came into our territory.

Everyone in our camp was talking about the Gray Ghost. Some thought the tall powerfully built Indian was a real man. Others thought he was a Spirit since he wouldn't let anyone come close to him. Everyone had a different opinion about who he was, where he came from and why he was in our territory. But nobody considered him to be an enemy.

After awhile, I got tired of all that talk and decided to go and find the Gray Ghost myself. I rode my pony in ever widening circles for four days until I found the tracks of a horse carrying a heavy rider going north. Since the tracks were fresh, I decided to gallop after the Gray Ghost as fast as I could. My plan worked, and it worked so quickly that I didn't know what to do when I came charging up to the smiling man.

But when the Gray Ghost held out his hands in a gesture of friendship, I felt my heart filling up with a strange and wonderful kind of love.

My love was not the kind that a woman feels when she wants to take a man into her wickiup....

My love was the kind that a person feels for a wise teacher, or a magnificent mountain or a star-filled sky.

We spent many afternoons together. It didn't matter that we couldn't speak the same language. True friends can understand each other without words. The Gray One helped me understand that I wanted to grow up to be wise and strong so I could help my people. And I learned that he was a chief who had come to our territory to strengthen and refresh his spirit in our Sacred Warm Springs.

One morning I woke up sensing something strange was going to happen. I looked into the direction of the rising sun and saw 12 warriors guarding a wagon carrying two BEAUTIFUL women. One of the women looked the way White Changing Woman appears to us when she is young. The other woman looked the way the deity appears to us when she is in the next stage of her life. Her face was lined with the softness and grace of wisdom.

I was sad, but not surprised, to see the Gray Ghost riding in front of the wagon since all 12 of the warriors had handsome hawk-shaped noses that looked like his.

Then something happened to lift my spirits. The Gray One turned and called out to me in a language that I could understand. He said, "Victorio was born to be a great chief. And you, Lozen, were born to ride with him."

I never saw the Gray Ghost again. But I did see the two beautiful women a year later. They came to my puberty ceremony to tell me that I must remain unmarried so I could serve my people with my whole heart. They told me how to make this Two-Sided Woman medicine robe and taught me this prayer.

> *"Sun, I am not a man,*
> *But you have given me a strong body, a courageous heart, and a powerful spirit.*
> *For this I thank You.*
> *I am Lozen – your Sun-blessed, far-seeing warrior woman.*

Water, though I am only a woman,
You have given me the power of healing,
the power of vision and the power of plants.
For this I thank You.
I am Lozen – your Water-blessed, far-see-
ing medicine woman."

Many men were disappointed by my determination not to marry. They couldn't do anything about it. Victorio was their chief. And Victorio supported my decision. He said, "Lozen is my right hand, braver than most, and cunning in strategy. Lozen will not marry because she was chosen by Ussen to be a shield to her people."

My brother always put the needs of his people before his own desires. He tried to avoid getting into conflicts with the Americans because he hoped they'd let us stay on our own land if we didn't cause them any trouble.

That changed when soldiers murdered Red Sleeves while he was carrying a white flag of truce. My brother agreed to lead the chief's sons on the warpath after he heard about the way the cowardly soldiers had cut up the great chief's body and boiled his head.

Victorio's face filled with rage as he said, "The white eyes have NO truth or honor in their hearts!

We can NEVER trust them. How can they call us savages when they are the ones who enslave our women and children, sell our scalps and LAUGH as they throw Apache babies into campfires!"

Victorio led us to many victories because he knew how to think like a mountain lion. He knew how to strike and then fade back into the mountains. And he knew how to inspire us to fight like wildcats!

We fought for revenge. But that's not the only reason we fought. We fought to preserve our way of life. We fought because whenever the government forced us to live on reservations our babies and children would die like flies! We fought to keep our spirits from shriveling up and dying. We fought to survive!

White Changing Woman gave me three Powers. She gave me Horse Power so I could steal many horses. She gave me Plant Power so I could heal wounds and help babies come into the world. And she gave me Enemy Power so I could help my people escape from our enemies.

She told me that I could locate the direction of our enemies if I would hold out my hands and turn slowly around in a circle while I chanted these words:

"In this world, Ussen has Power.

This Power He has granted me for the good of my people.

This I see as if I was standing on the highest mountain looking down on the world in every direction.

This I feel as though I held something in the palms of my hands – something that tingles.

This power is mine to use – but only for the good of my people."

If the enemy was coming from this direction, and I was facing that way, my hands would get warm. And if the enemy was close, my hands would get hot!

My Enemy Power made it possible for our band to move freely from one mountain range to the next. We did that even though we were being pursued by thousands of Mexican and American soldiers. And my enemy power helped me keep my brother safe.

But since I'm a Two-Sided Woman, there were times when I had to leave the warriors to take care of the more helpless members of our band.

Victorio was surrounded and killed in Mexico during one of those times.

Nana and I did not pause to mourn for my brother and the 62 warriors and all the women and children who died with him. We led our remaining 15 warriors and a group of Mescalero Apaches on a bloody rampage of revenge. And then...and THEN. . . we joined forces with Geronimo!

But tonight is not the time for me to think about those battles and how the army used Apache Scouts to track us down.

Since I am a Two-Sided Woman, I must push aside my desire to die as a warrior and pour all of my Power and strength into the healing side of myself. I will use that Power and strength to help my people learn how to endure captivity. I will tell them spirit-strengthening stories. I will tell them stories that they can pass on to their children.

I will tell them about our Apache warriors. I will tell them how our warriors kept our land free for hundreds and hundreds of years.

And then, whenever I look up and see a starfilled sky and feel Ussen's Power surging inside me, I will remember how it feels to be a STRONG Apache warrior.

[The End]

Background

Emma Lee

Drawing by Carol Sletten after a photograph

The Life Journey of Emma (Batchelor) Lee (French)

Born in Uckfield, England (1)
Traveled to Liverpool (2) to take
ship to America

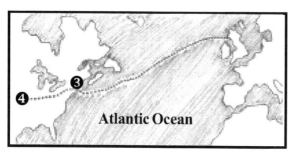

Landed in Boston (3)
Took train to Iowa City (4)

Pushed a handcart 1,300 miles to Salt Lake
City (5)

Moved to Harmony, near scene of
Mountain Meadows Massacre (6)
Moved to Lee's Ferry (7)
Moved to Winslow and other towns in
White Mountains (8)

Emma Lee Timeline

1836 Born Emma Batchelor in Uckfield, England.

1856 Converted to Mormonism and took passage to Boston, continuing on by train to Iowa City.

1856 Pulled a handcart for 1,300 miles to Salt Lake City, Utah.

1857 Future husband John D. Lee and other Mormons involved in massacre of a wagon train at Mountain Meadows in southern Utah.

1858 Emma married John D. Lee and moved to Harmony in southern Utah, not far from the scene of the recent massacre.

1859 Officers began searching for Lee because of his role in the massacre and he went into part-time hiding near their home.

1870 As the investigation of the massacre continued, the Lee family moved from Harmony to a remote site near Kanab, Utah, where they set up a sawmill.

1872 The family migrated to the Colorado River in Arizona where they established Lee's Ferry.

1875 Lee was tried for murder in the massacre, but the trial resulted in a hung jury. Emma operated the ferry throughout the period of Lee's trials and after his execution.

1876 Lee's second trial resulted in conviction.

1877 Lee executed by firing squad at Mountain Meadows.

1879 Emma sold the ferry location to Mormon church leaders and left for Arizona's White Mountains, marrying prospector Frank French when the couple arrived in Snowflake. They moved to the community of Sunset near Winslow, but were denied water for irrigation and moved on to Forestdale on the White Mountain Apache reservation.

1882 The family's farm was burned during the Cibecue Uprising and they retreated to Fort Apache before moving to Holbrook.

1887 The family moved to Winslow where she was known as Doctor Grandma French, serving the community's medical needs with herbal medicine.

1888 Daughter Vicky committed suicide, distraught over guilt placed on the family for the massacre.

1897 Emma died in Winslow.

Mormon Religion

Like Islam, Judaism and other Christian denominations, Mormon beliefs trace their origin to the writings of Hebrew scholars in the Middle East thousands of years ago. As Mohammed took the concept of the creator God and preached doctrines to the Arabs, Joseph Smith expanded religious teachings to include God's interaction with people in North America.

Smith said that in 1823 an angel led him to golden plates buried in a stone box in Upstate New York. He told followers that he used a stone to translate the words from "Reformed Egyptian" and copied down the accounts of God's people in North America. After finishing the book, he returned the plates to the angel.

The *Book of Mormon* presents itself as the writings, around 400 A.D., of a man named Mormon and his son Moroni, who compiled the book from earlier works. It covers a period from 2200 B.C. to 421 A.D. and tells of two groups of people migrating to North America. The Jaredites leave the Tower of Babel around 2200 B.C. and travel to the New World on barges. Their civilization thrives for centuries but eventually dies out. A second group leaves Jerusalem shortly before the city is captured by Babylon in 586 B.C. They journey across Arabia and take a ship to North America. This latter group divides into Nephites, the followers of God, and Lamenites, ancestors to Native Americans.

Jesus visits the New World shortly after his resurrection and creates a peace, but it breaks down after a few hundred years and the Lamenites eliminate the Nephites.

Just as the Bible teaches doctrine in its accounts of Hebrew history, the Book of Mormon explains tenents of Latter-day Saint belief. Humans existed prior to birth as spirits who were children of God. Jesus was the oldest of these children of God. The child spirits were given bodies so they could experience the world and become more like God. Everyone will be resurrected into a Kingdom of God, but only the most devout will make it to the highest kingdom. Below the heaven for Mormons is one for other Christians and Jews, with others inhabiting the bottom tier.

Mormons believe that the priesthood of early Christianity died out with the martyrdom of the Apostles, and that it was only restored through angels visiting Joseph Smith. They believe there are multiple universes, each has a God who governs his own world.

As Smith went from being a publisher of an obscure book to the leader of a growing church, Mormon literature was expanded to include the Doctrine and Covenants as well as the Pearl of Great Price. When Smith was killed by a mob in Carthage, Illinois, he became a martyr like the prophets in his text.

Somewhat like the Pope, Mormon leaders are believed to have the gift of divine revelation. In 1978, black men, who had previously been excluded from the priesthood, were granted full participation in the church through a revelation received by President Spencer Kimball.

Polygamy

Mormons came to polygamy in stages, the first step being secret extra marriages enjoyed by Prophet Joseph Smith, perhaps as early as 1831. The "principle" was gradually extended to a small inner-circle within the Latter-day Saints' community of Nauvoo, Illinois. When the practice of polygamy was exposed, it rent the church. Smith attempted to explain new doctrines covering his behavior, but they were met with skepticism, particularly by his first wife.

Polygamy played a major role in the arrest and murder of Smith by a mob in 1844. When he was gone, leadership of the church fell to Brigham Young, who had been in the inner-circle and had multiple wives.

Mormons looking for support for their practice found precedents in other cultures. Affluent Moslems could have up to four wives. Wealthy Chinese had concubines, and primitive societies throughout the world allowed polygamy. They even found occasional glimpses of toleration of polygamy in Europe. The Catholic Church did not prohibit the practice until after 600 A.D. and encouraged polygamy in Germany after the 30 Years War in the 1600s because so many men had died in the conflict. On the American continent, Native Americans, who had a special role in Mormon belief, practiced polygamy.

Young didn't expect the practices of his church to be subject to the laws of the United States when he moved followers to the Mountain West. He publicly declared for polygamy and married 55 women. But with the Mexican War, Manifest Destiny quickly caught up with the Mormon migration. Utah and surrounding areas were taken into American jurisdiction.

As with the Moslems and Chinese, the practice of plural marriage within the Mormon community was limited to the wealthy. About 80 percent of Mormons remained monogamous while well-off men took a new wife every five to ten years. Only the highest church officials took many dozens of wives.

Accounts of how the practice actually worked are somewhat mixed. Children have given accounts of the positive aspects of being raised and cared for by more than one mother. Other accounts indicate wives were not always happy to have additional women join their families.

The first attempt by Congress in 1862 to outlaw the practice wasn't enforced because the government was tied up in the Civil War. Another law passed in 1882 made polygamy a felony and the government began a more serious prosecution which disrupted the economic and social structure of many Mormon families.

Polygamists played a cat-and-mouse game of hiding wives or fled to Mexico. Prosecutions, which started in Utah, extended to Arizona where a number of leaders of the church were sent to prison.

In 1890, Church President Wilford Woodruff, who had previously spent time hiding from federal prosecution in Arizona, realized that the burdens and risks of polygamy were too much for the church to carry. He decided that Mormons living in the United States should obey the law and have only one wife. The decision was cast as an accommodation to local law but did not prohibit polygamy in areas, such as Mexico, where it was not against any law.

The change in official church position allowed Utah to be admitted to the Union as the 46th state in 1896. Some Mormons in the United States kept their multiple wives even after Woodruff's announcement and prosecutions continued into the 20th century.

The Handcart Song

-- Carol Sletten

FOR SOME MUST PUSH,
AND SOME MUST PULL,
AS WE GO MARCHING UP THE HILL!
SO MERRILY ON OUR WAY
WE GO, UNTIL WE REACH
THE VALLEY O!

Missionaries taught this to Mormon converts, who sang it
with much enthusiasm while they were waiting to cross the
ocean and head across the continent to their promised land
in Utah.

Handcarts

Mormons, having been repeatedly run out of substantial settlements across the Midwest, were determined to hang onto their territory in Utah. To do this, they felt they needed to rapidly increase their population by converting and bringing over Europeans, especially those from the lower classes in England and Scandinavia.

But although the missionaries were successful in converting and moving thousands across the ocean and on to the Midwest, they faced a tremendous obstacle in getting them through the untamed wilderness to Utah. Deeply in debt from the ship and railroad passage to Iowa City, the immigrants were still 1,300 miles from Salt Lake City. The usual method for moving farther west was a wagon and oxen, which cost $300, well beyond the means of most converts. Though a fund had been created to loan money to the immigrants for the trip, the cost, even without purchasing a wagon and ox team, was already so high that some immigrants were never able to pay off their debts.

The idea of using handcarts came from seeing prospectors pushing wheelbarrows through Utah in the California gold rush of 1849. So necessity and religious zeal turned an expedient for a few crazed able-bodied men seeking gold into a life-and-death struggle for thousands of people, including many women and children.

Mormon handcarts looked like baggage carts used at 19th century train stations. The box was about three feet wide and five feet long, with low sides and open at the top. They had two wheels, four and a half feet in diameter, set apart at the same distance as wagon wheels so carts could follow existing ruts on the trail. The wheels were relatively light with thin wooden spokes. But unlike a wheelbarrow, the handles extended forward. A crossbar at the end of the handles allowed the pioneers to lift and push the cart. Some had canvas tops, which made them look like miniature covered wagons.

In addition to allowing space for two people at the crossbar, others could push from the rear or even be harnessed to pull the cart. The device, which weighed 65 pounds empty, carried 17 pounds of baggage per traveler. Food and, sometimes a disabled member of the party, could increase the load to several hundred pounds. The carts, which cost only $10 to $20, were often built quickly from green lumber and broke down as they creaked toward Utah.

On June 9, 1856, the first handcart company left Iowa City with another following two days later. Each company of approximately 300 people had a couple of wagons drawn by teams to carry additional food, tents and supplies. The Mormon leaders seemed to expect miraculous results and divine protection for their enterprise. But mortality far outnumbered miracles, particularly when the steep mountain grades were covered by snow. Bitterly cold temperatures closed in on the companies if they were caught on the trail when fall turned to winter. Though church leaders had predicted the companies would travel up to 30 miles a day, they averaged only nine miles a day even when crossing the relatively flat terrain of Iowa, the easiest and first part of their long journey.

Children were herded in a single group ahead of the company while their parents toiled with the carts in the rear. Many died from starvation crossing Nebraska. Re-supply wagons sent east from Salt Lake City met the first companies near the Nebraska-Wyoming line, giving each company 1,000 pounds of flour. Another re-supply occurred a few weeks later. Finally, on Sept. 25, 1856, people from Salt Lake City, including church President Brigham Young, rode out to meet the first party of pioneers camped just a few miles north of the city. Though records are incomplete, of the first group of 272, about 33 dropped out and at least 12 died.

As immigrants continued to arrive on the East Coast, additional handcart companies were launched from Iowa City. A group from Wales had to reduce rations to a quarter-pound of flour per adult per day as they headed to Utah. That was not enough to sustain life, particularly for those doing the heavy work of pushing and pulling the carts. But those difficulties and tragedies didn't prevent the other handcart companies from heading West as the season progressed.

The hardest journey was that of the Martin Company, which started too late in the season and got trapped in the snows of Wyoming. Six to eight deaths occurred each night as rations were cut to four ounces of flour per day for an adult. One night 19 members of the party died. In all, 220 of the 575 members of the party perished on the trail, the worst disaster in the history of Western migration in the U.S.

The Martin Company left the Omaha area on Aug. 25. The first snowstorm hit them on Oct. 19, the very same day that they were in Wyoming crossing the swift current of the Platte River. They were further threatened when the re-supply wagons that were scheduled to meet them apparently gave their flour to other travelers. The progress of the handcarts slowed in the deepening snow and finally, at Red Buttes in Wyoming, they stopped, unable to move on because of cold, exhaustion, hunger and snow.

Emma Batchelor (Lee) was in the Martin company at this point, having dropped out of the Willie company when she was ordered to leave behind a brass kettle holding her belongings. The young and strong Emma was a welcome addition to the company. She acted as a midwife for a woman who gave birth to a child and pushed her on a cart for two days as she recovered. Emma was always careful to take her shoes and stockings off before crossing a stream and dried and warmed her feet carefully before continuing. She carried a little boy over each stream, being careful to keep his feet dry.

When Brigham Young learned of the late departure of the Martin and Willie companies, he exhorted the people of Salt Lake City to immediately go to the rescue. Despite crop failures in Utah, flour was loaded into wagons and driven east to meet the unfortunate companies. The rescue parties were able to supply food, but not cure the problems of cold and exhaustion. The Willie company lost 15 members in a single day after they were "rescued." The Martin company suffered more than half of its fatalities after meeting up with the rescue party from Salt Lake City. Many survivors were maimed by the experience.

After the first brutal year, only five additional handcart companies came to Utah. Though the advance of the railroad across Missouri made the journey shorter, and rules were changed to make the trip safer, it was still a dangerous, hungry trek. The last two companies made the journey in 1860 with the loss of only one life.

Mountain Meadows

Just as generations of white settlers took land from Native Americans whom they considered inferior, Americans used religious differences to justify the way they drove Mormons from their homes and stole their land. Before the Mormons got to their sanctuary in Utah, they had been driven from substantial homes, businesses and farms which they had created with much labor in Kirtland, Ohio; Jackson County, Missouri; and Nauvoo, Illinois.

The Mormon War started in Missouri when the state militia, called out because of rising violence, attacked Mormons at Haun's Mill, killing 18 men and boys who believed they had negotiated an armistice. In addition, 1,200 members of the church were forced to flee their homes into the November cold. The governor declared that Mormons were enemies and "must be exterminated or driven from the State." After their property was confiscated, the Latter-day Saints went to Illinois and founded the town of Nauvoo along the Mississippi River. Though the confrontation with Missouri continued when one of Smith's bodyguards tried to assassinate the governor of that state.

In Illinois, the Mormons were a growing and feared presence. The population of Nauvoo reached 12,000 in 1844, rivaling Chicago which had fewer than 5,000 people in the 1840 census. Tensions mounted as Smith's embrace of polygamy became known. No longer content to serve as mayor of Nauvoo under a state charter, the prophet proclaimed an earthly Kingdom of God and said his new theocracy would "swallow up" the state. He petitioned Congress to create a Mormon army of 100,000 volunteers to protect a vast swath of the West from Texas to Oregon. Smith was crowned "King of Israel" and ran for president of the United States.

Hostilities in Illinois boiled over in 1844 when Smith propositioned the wives of two of his followers, who then created a newspaper to expose the Prophet's doctrine of polygamy. When the Prophet ordered his militia to destroy the newspaper and its press, a warrant was issued for his arrest and he responded by declaring martial law. A nearby newspaper proclaimed, "War and extermination is inevitable!" Smith surrendered, went to jail and became a martyr to his people after he and his brother were killed by a mob.

Brigham Young became the new leader. He tried to strengthen Nauvoo and remain in Illinois, but when mobs systematically burned Mormon homes and chased the Saints off their farms, Young decided to "leave the United States" and set up a Kingdom of God in the Rocky Mountains. After he chose his head clerk, John D. Lee, to organize the trek West, Temple rites were performed to make Lee the second of Young's 38 adopted sons. Lee also took a temple oath to avenge the blood of Joseph and Hyrum Smith and other Mormons killed in Missouri.

After retreating to the Rocky Mountains and building Salt Lake City, the Mormons remained committed to "vengeance on the wicked nation" of the United States. They often stated that if they were given 10 years to build their new country, they would be so powerful that they would never be driven out again. After America seized the area in the Mexican War, Young successfully petitioned Congress to make Utah a territory. President Millard Fillmore named Young as the territory's governor. The Prophet also became commissioner of Indian affairs in Utah and appointed the federal Indian agents. Because the Mormons believed Indians were descendants of Israelites who had migrated to America before Christ, Native Americans played a special role in the LDS plans. The agents told the Indians that Mormons were their friends and that

Americans were their enemies. They allowed the natives to steal livestock from Americans traveling through Utah so the Mormons could sell it.

From Salt Lake City, Mormons, including John D. Lee, set out to colonize southern Utah. They were a hardcore group of long-time believers. Juanita Brooks, a Mormon who wrote *The Mountain Meadows Massacre*, said most had been through the persecutions of Missouri and Illinois and their bishop was a survivor of the Haun's Mill massacre. They made friends with the local Southern Paiutes by protecting them from the slave raids of Mexicans and Utes.

The Paiutes had long suffered from American travelers. John C. Fremont's men killed several members of their tribe without provocation. The wagon trains had also destroyed their edible plants and diminished game. Brigham Young appointed John D. Lee as "Farmer to the Indians," a federal salaried position responsible for teaching the Indians agriculture and maintaining peace between the Southern Paiutes and non-Mormon emigrants passing through Utah on their way to California.

Meanwhile, federal officers were having a hard time in Utah. Some died mysteriously. Others, who fled, spread news of Mormon hostility to the United States. While the Latter-day Saints saw their efforts to frustrate federal officials as keeping their territory in the hands of God's Prophet, the federal government took a very dim view of attempts to subvert its authority. When renewed accounts of polygamy surfaced, American hostility toward Utah increased.

Mormon belligerence toward the United States government also increased. The Territorial Legislature took jurisdiction away from the federal district court so that criminal and civil matters were decided in Mormon-controlled "probate" courts. John D. Lee said that since Mormons were persecuted, members of the LDS church were justified in stealing from gentiles. Brigham Young preached repeatedly about a divine revelation that told him the late President Zachery Taylor was in hell and that other federal officials would join him there. Every able-bodied Mormon man was mustered into the militia, which drilled and prepared for war.

When Indians massacred a railroad survey crew and the federal government sent troops to investigate, the bawdy behavior of the troops stationed in Salt Lake City furthered antagonisms. Though the leader of the army expedition, Col. Edward Steptoe, had been appointed governor of Utah, he left the territory without taking the post. That left Brigham Young in charge. When an Indian chief told a group of his warriors to take responsibility for the massacre, they were convicted of manslaughter by a Mormon jury but were allowed to promptly walk away from prison to rejoin their tribe.

When white outlaws disguised as Indians, sometimes with the help of actual Indians, stole livestock from wagon trains, stories circulated, and were sometimes proved, that the whites were Mormons.

A two-year drought and a plague of grasshoppers in the mid-1850s set the stage for a fervid reformation within the Mormon Church. Young preached the doctrine of "Blood Atonement." Though the precise meaning was complex, it became a justification for killing people on the outs with the church leadership.

After rumors spread that an army was being assembled in the East to attack Utah, hostility to outsiders ratcheted to even higher levels. The Utah Legislature passed a law saying they would choose which federal laws to obey and that they would reject any federal officials whom they considered to be immoral.

One more incident served to raise tensions to the boiling point. Apostle Parley Pratt, a high-ranking member of the Mormon Church, had married a woman who left her children and a husband behind in the East. When Pratt helped her return to recover her children, the woman's first husband tracked down the missionary and brutally murdered him in Arkansas. That created even more ill-feeling between the people of Arkansas and Utah. Newspapers reported the murder and openly speculated on whether Mormons disguised as Indians would attack wagon trains in Utah in retaliation.

Unable to tackle the complex issues of slavery, President James Buchanan sought to turn public attention to the rebellious Mormon territory. He appointed a new governor and ordered an army to march on Utah. Brigham Young, gathering thousands at a camp meeting, preached that the conflict with the United States would usher in the end of the world and the next coming of Christ. His people were stunned to hear that they were considered to be in rebellion, and that the United States was going to war with them. Mormons considered the Constitution of the United States a divinely inspired document, even though they felt obligated to help church leaders frustrate the government's officials. Having been personally chased and burned out of their homes several times, they resolved to torch their own properties rather than have their communities fall into the hands of invaders.

Meanwhile in Arkansas, Alexander Fancher was putting together a wagon train. He was a wealthy descendant of French Protestants who had fled to America in the 1600s. His uncle was a friend of Abraham Lincoln. His wife and nine children made up the core of the train, but through relatives and other connections it expanded to140 members when combined with other wagon trains. Two-thirds were women and children. They purchased a large number of cattle to sell at high prices to hungry miners in California.

Fancher had made two previous trips to California, traveling through Salt Lake city in 1850 and making the second trip in 1854.

This time Fancher's Arkansas wagon train arrived in Salt Lake City just as war hysteria in Utah reached fever pitch. Apostle George A. Smith, a cousin of the slain prophet, rode ahead into southern Utah, reviewing the militia and encouraging the settlers to resist the U.S. Army. Orders telling the militia to be ready to fight and to deny grain to emigrant wagon trains put men on edge and increased the sense of military emergency. The "Minute Men" were ordered to pay "careful attention" to opportunities to obtain arms and ammunition from passing wagon trains.

"It would sweeten death to a man to know that he should lay down his life in defense of freedom and the kingdom of God, rather than to longer bow to the cruelty of mobs, even when the mob have the name of being legalized by the nation," John Taylor said in a sermon to a large congregation. Taylor, an Englishman who later succeeded Brigham Young as church leader, had been personally converted to the LDS faith by the slain Apostle Parley Pratt.

Mormons throughout Utah sang this hymn:

Up, awake, ye defenders of Zion,
The foe's at the door of your homes.
Let each heart be the heart of a lion
Unyielding and proud as he roams.
Remember the wrongs of Missouri
Forget not the fate of Nauvoo
When the God-hating foe is before you
Stand firm and be faithful and true.

The sentiment was at least as high among the approaching federal troops. Brooks quotes a Captain Jesse A. Gove as writing, "If the Mormons will only fight, their days are numbered. We shall sweep them from the face of the earth and Mormonism in Utah shall cease."

In a situation somewhat similar to the intemperate words of Henry II that led to the slaying of Saint Thomas Becket at Canterbury, the bluster of Apostle George Smith and other Mormon leaders was about to fall on the ears of a remarkably efficient true believer who could transform angry words into deadly action.

Smith specifically asked John D. Lee if he thought the settlers and Indians would destroy a wagon train if it "made threats against our people and bragging of the part they took in helping to kill our Prophets." Lee answered that any emigrants would be wiped out if they had been making threats against the Mormon people. In fact, Lee told the apostle that any wagon train would be destroyed unless Brigham Young sent orders to let them pass.

There continues to be dispute on whether Brigham Young actually sent orders to attack the wagon train. Lee said he believed Smith was delivering Young's orders.

The Mormon historian Juanita Brooks cites the sermons and other communications of Apostle Smith as setting the stage for the massacre. She quotes William Adams as writing, "The year 1857 was a trying time for the Saints, extermination from our homes, fleeing to the mountains, destruction of our property all were calculated upon. We were preparing for the worst, caching our flour in the mountains. The Saints in the north were moving south ready to put the torch to their homes."

Meanwhile, in Salt Lake City, Young preached a sermon saying he would close down transcontinental travel because of the Army's pending attack. He said wagon trains had only been successful because he prevented the Indians from attacking, and he would end his protection. California newspapers carried accounts of wagon trains being attacked by Mormons and Indians.

Reports spread that the widow of Apostle Parley Pratt recognized members of the Fancher party as being present at the murder of her husband in Arkansas. This report served to identify, in the public mind, the Fancher party as an invading force that must be stopped. And the wagon train had repeated conflicts with the local Mormons as it traveled through southern Utah, usually because its large cattle herd ate grass locals needed to save for winter pasture.

Ill feeling increased when Mormon apostates joined the wagon train in hopes of getting safely out of Utah. False rumors were spread that the emigrants had poisoned a spring to kill Indians. Brooks cites persistent reports that the Fancher party deliberately antagonized the Mormons. The travelers named an ox Brigham Young and loudly cursed him, they popped the heads off farmers' chickens with bull whips and grazed their cattle in Mormon fields, according to Brooks. She apparently believed the story that one emigrant claimed to have the gun that killed Joseph Smith. "Whether all the reports were true is not so important as the fact that the people believed that they were true," she wrote.

Brigham Young and other Mormon leaders, bent on closing transcontinental travel to gain leverage with the United States, met with Indian chiefs in Salt Lake City and told them they could have the cattle belonging to wagon trains moving though the country. Four hundred head of cattle had already been stolen from a wagon train on a more northerly route, and attention turned to the Fancher party moving through southern Utah.

Orders to have the Indians attack the wagon train, according to *Blood of the Prophets* author Will Bagley, came down from Militia leader William Dame to Cedar City church leader Issac Haight and finally to John D. Lee. Haight spoke at a Cedar City church meeting, recounting the history of aggression against the Mormon Church. He said he had been driven from his home for the last time. Some accounts say participants voted to kill the emigrants. Mormons gathered at a camp well-armed and then dressed as Indians while Lee and the Paiutes, at a second camp, prepared for the attack.

In explaining the tragedy, Mormon author Brooks wrote, "Records make it doubly clear that the massacre at Mountain Meadows was committed by a military group under military orders, by men fired by what was later called 'The Spirit of the Times.' Spurred on by the inflammatory speeches of their Church leaders, their own determination not to be driven again, their private vows to avenge the blood of the Prophets, the promises in their Patriarchal Blessings that they would be permitted to do so – all these carried some weight. But military orders placed each man where he was to do his duty. After it was over, not a man of them would ever be the same again, either in his own heart or in the eyes of his neighbors."

The Fancher party arrived at Mountain Meadows in southern Utah, an oasis on the desolate wagon road to California. Its lush grass allowed wagon trains to feed and restore their livestock to such an extent that it made the trip possible.

The attackers sneaked into the camp before dawn on Monday, Sept. 7, 1857, first stealing livestock and then returning to fire into the camp at dawn. Ten to 15 immigrants were killed or wounded in the first barrage, but others quickly grabbed guns and returned fire, forcing the attackers to retreat. Wagons were circled and dirt was shoveled up under them to build a crude fortification.

After suffering unexpected casualties, the Paiutes began

to lose interest. Lee realized that the Indians would not be able to take the fortified camp and went for reinforcements, more Indians and Mormon militia. Mormons in Cedar City decided to send a messenger to Brigham Young for instructions. Meanwhile, Mormons began gathering at the Meadows to renew the attack. A detachment of the Nauvoo Legion arrived on Tuesday afternoon and at least one hundred Mormon men from all over southern Utah eventually joined the fight. The number of Indians engaged is uncertain, with estimates ranging from 40 to several hundred.

By Tuesday, the Indians were leaving the battle site, often taking a few cattle. Lee admitted to participating in an attack on Tuesday night, remembering a hail of bullets coming from the emigrants. He claimed that he was a noncombatant.

On Wednesday night, two men from the wagon train tried to sneak through the surrounding enemies to get help from other wagon trains behind them on the trail. Both men were killed.

As the battle dragged on for five days, the women and children stayed in defensive pits dug by the emigrants. The smell of dead animals added to the terror and they remained cut off from the spring, which was just outside their defensive lines.

Meanwhile, an advance party of the Army arrived in Salt Lake City and met with Young, whose assessment of the threat caused by the United States was apparently downgraded. When the rider arrived from the south asking for instructions, Young claims to have responded with orders to let the emigrants go in peace.

Three emigrants who escaped the scene of the massacre to try to get help were tracked down and killed.

By Friday morning, there were fewer than two dozen men left to defend the circled wagons and they were almost out of ammunition. The failure of the Indian attack and the presence of Mormons among the attackers made decisions difficult for the Mormon leaders who could not afford to leave witnesses. The Mormons approached the wagon fort under a white flag and offered to give the party protection from the Indians and safe passage to Cedar City if they would lay down their arms. Out of options, the party accepted the plan.

"The Mormon officers carefully segregated the emigrant families into three groups – men[;] women and children[;] and infants and wounded – and their supposed protectors marched them north from the camp," says *Blood of the Prophets*. "In early twilight at the rim of the Great Basin, the militia shot down the unarmed men. Young whites disguised in paint and feathers and a small band of native freebooters rushed from ambush to murder the terrified women and children. More than two dozen adult women and fifty children, ranging in age from infancy to eighteen years, died in the assault. The Mormons and their allies killed everyone except seventeen children, not over six years of age. Some of them were painfully wounded, but their 'innocent blood' and presumed inability to tell their story spared them from the general slaughter."

The younger children were taken in a wagon to a nearby ranch and then most of them on to Cedar City where they were placed in foster homes. Lee's efficiency in turning political bluster into more than 100 mutilated corpses shocked and sickened the militia leaders who had approached the undertaking with false bravado. Standing at the site of the massacre, the officers were overcome by horror and began to deny their role in ordering the massacre, according to *Blood of the Prophets*.

A few days after the events, two non-Mormons were with a group of Mormon freighters who passed the horrific scene, where the bodies were still unburied. The freighters sought to hide the killings from their non-Mormon guests. They passed the site at night and asked the non-Mormons to stay low in the wagons, supposedly to protect them from Indians. The travelers saw enough to provide some of the first accounts of the massacre to the outside world, talking to newspapers when they reached California.

While the Mormons were reasonably good at keeping their secret, the Indians were not. After the story reached an Indian agent, Dr. Garland Hurt, in northern Utah, he sent a man to secretly investigate the scene of the massacre. When he received the report, Hurt escaped from Utah , traveling for 27 days through the wilderness to reach an Army detachment and tell them what had happened.

Wagon trains that followed the Fancher party that season were robbed of their livestock by "Indians" but not killed, according to *Blood of the Prophets*. The loot from the Fancher party caused disputes. Lee claimed he took possession of the cattle on direction of Brigham Young and cared for them for the benefit of the Indians. Other property was taken to Cedar City and auctioned, while jewelry of the victims was worn openly in Salt Lake City.

Lee reported on the massacre in person to Brigham Young, who, realizing it was a disaster for the church, encouraged Lee to blame the Indians. Young's actions were both cautious and reckless. In his accounts as a federal government Indian agent, he billed the federal government for expenses for the militia and Indians involved in the massacre, and even for goods taken from the murdered emigrants.

When newspaper accounts of the massacre circulated in California, Young wrote to the newspapers blaming the emigrants for provoking the Indians. A public mass meeting in Los Angeles blamed Mormons for the massacre. Newspapers called out for revenge. The "Utah War" heated up with the Nauvoo Legion burning supply wagons and running off stock belonging to the Army units advancing from the East toward the territory.

As tensions increased, church leaders ordered Mormons to quickly evacuate their settlement of San Bernardino, California, which forced them to sell their prime property at low prices. And then their trek to Utah through the still-visible carnage at Mountain Meadows confused, outraged and alarmed them. The government ordered all armed groups of Mormons to give up their weapons, and many LDS leaders were indicted on charges of treason. An Indian attack on a Mormon settlement in Idaho called into question the church's strategy of using Indian allies to fight the United States Army. After President Buchanan continued to dispatch more troops to the territory, Brigham Young decided to accept Buchanan's new territorial governor rather than fight.

When the continued presence of young children from the wagon train in the hands of Mormon families fueled and added credibility to the story of the Mountain Meadows massacre, volunteer military companies sprang up across Northern California determined to attack the Mormons. Newspapers from California reached the East and outrage spread, particularly in the Ozarks among the families of the slain. Congress took up the issue and demanded action.

When a Mormon investigation got underway, Lee handed out gold to the investigators, who exonerated him. But as the inquiry continued and no one was willing to take blame, a line was added to the final report saying Lee and a few other white men were present during parts of the massacre. The report said investigators did not know why Lee was there or what he did, but it clearly set him up as the scapegoat.

A federal judge called a grand jury, but Mormon jurors and a sympathetic prosecutor frustrated the inquiry. The Army went to Mountain Meadows, buried the dead and prepared a report. Soon the killings were on the front page of *Harper's Weekly*. Thirty-eight suspected killers were indicted but never brought to trial. It was estimated that 40 percent of the white men living within 150 miles of the massacre had taken part. The children were recovered by the government with the help of the Army. Lee submitted a bill for the care of little Charles Fancher and the ransom he had supposedly paid to Indians to rescue the child. The children, some with graphic accounts of the murder of their parents, were returned to Arkansas. Brigham Young feared lynching by federal authorities and Apostle Wilford Woodruff protected church documents because he feared that Salt Lake City would be burned. But immediate action was delayed by an inept governor and hostility to federal officials as well as various legal technicalities. As the years dragged by, the communities of southern Utah began to dwindle. The causes of the depopulation were complex, but many left to avoid the stigma of the Mountain Meadow Massacre or actual prosecution.

The Civil War interrupted the investigation. Albert Sidney Johnston, who had led federal efforts in Utah, became the second-ranking officer of the Confederacy. Dying at the Battle of Shiloh, Johnston was the highest ranking officer killed during the war. Gen. James Carleton, the other high-ranking federal general involved in the Utah matter, went to the Union side and protected California, Arizona and New Mexico from the Confederates. By the time the war ended, John D. Lee was the leading suspect in the massacre. (See Lee's life story in the next chapter). Brooks agrees that Lee played a leading role, but points out he was not at the church meeting where it was decided to make the attack, nor was he the militia leader who ordered the attack, nor was he even present when the first shots were fired. Lee took the blame for many.

John D. Lee

Adapted from an 1888 etching

John D. Lee

Though John D. Lee was descended from well-to-do families in the frontier fort town of Kaskaskia, Illinois, crime and alcoholism made his childhood very difficult.

The chain of events started before he was born when his mother, Elizabeth, was living with her first husband. A man broke into their home at night, killed the husband and severely injured Lee's half sister. The intruder attempted to kill the mother who had witnessed the murder, leaving her permanently disabled.

Elizabeth survived to marry into a very prominent family. Her second husband, Ralph Lee, was an Indian agent, prosperous businessman and descendant of the same Revolutionary War heroes as distant cousin Robert E. Lee, the Confederate general. He built a mansion for his new family but became an abusive alcoholic when their son John D. Lee was very small. After Elizabeth died of complications from injuries received during the break-in, a black French-speaking maid took care of little John D. Lee. When he was eight, the boy was sent to live with an aunt, who was also married to an abusive alcoholic. He was regularly beaten.

While others might have been broken by the experience, Lee's childhood left him extremely self-reliant, capable and ambitious, but obsessive in wanting to please those in authority.

Lee left at 16 to become a mail carrier, riding more than 100 miles on his route in the brutal Midwestern winter. He served in the Black Hawk War and worked on a steamship and for a merchant in Galena, Illinois, before marrying and becoming prosperous. Traveling Methodist, Baptist, Campbellite and Mormon preachers all held services in his large house. After listening to all of them, Lee decided that the Book of Mormon was true. He sold his property to join the Mormons in their colony in western Missouri where he was baptized into the church and set up a farm.

"Whatever duty was assigned me, I tried to discharge with a winning heart and ready hand," Lee wrote in his auto-biography. Lee joined a secret society called the Danites, whose members pledged to obey the church leaders, defend them from dissenters and protect the church. Lee said the penalty for failing to obey an order was death. The penalty was also imposed for disclosing the name of a member or any other information about the society. The group's name apparently came from ancient scripture, either from a prophecy in the Book of Daniel or the tribe of Samson. The Danites fought their first battle when a group of non-Mormons tried to prevent the Saints from voting in Gallatin, Missouri. The Danites won the battle by smashing their enemies' skulls with four-foot hickory clubs.

Though the Mormons were victorious in the battle of Gallatin, militias were soon formed to drive the Mormons out of Missouri. After LDS families left their farms to fort up in a couple of their towns, they began to use the tactics of guerrilla warfare. "I also soon saw that it was the natural inclination of men to steal, and convert to their own use that which others possessed," Lee wrote in his autobiography. "What perplexed me most was that religion had no power to subdue that passion in man, but drawn, the most devout men in our community acted like they had served a lifetime of evil, and were natural born thieves." He discovered that the Mormon ranks were filled with what he called "pulpit braves," willing to put on a show of bluster in meetings, but unwilling to face the enemy in the field. The Mormons burned and looted Gallatin and Lee witnessed, after another engagement, Apostle Parley Pratt shoot and attempt to kill a non-Mormon prisoner.

When an anti-Mormon faction overran a group of Mormons defending a mill and killed the survivors, the main body of Mormons at the community of Far West surrendered. They were forced to give up their real estate and personal property to pay the "expenses" of the attackers.

Lee then took his family to Illinois, where he was promoted into the Quorum of Seventy, a church leadership body, and served as a missionary in the Midwest while the Mormons built their new city at Nauvoo. The city sported a Masonic Lodge and Lee joined. But Nauvoo was not peaceful.

When Joseph Smith got in trouble for his doctrine of polygamy, he ordered the destruction of the local newspaper that denounced him. That led to the Prophet's arrest and murder by a mob. In the Quorum, Lee supported Brigham Young to succeed the martyred Joseph Smith, though he believed Young should defer to Smith's son when the boy came of age. Since Lee was chosen to become a bodyguard to Young, he moved into a house close to the new president's residence. Lee was also named general clerk and recorder of the Quorum, a sort of Mormon parliament. Lee claims in his autobiography that he was aware of secret murders of Young's enemies, carried out by Mormon policemen. But he said he did not participate in the killings, which also involved robberies of wealthy victims.

Lee married his second, third and fourth wives during that time, but resented Young taking one of his fiancées. Nonetheless, Lee was soon able to claim nine wives.

Lee said that Mormons continued to have conflicts with their neighbors in Illinois, often over cattle stealing. He was picked as a member of a small committee to get the Saints ready for a trip West, and sell Mormon property in Nauvoo. Lee went on a mission to Santa Fe with the Mormon Battalion, but when he returned he discovered that Brigham Young had not kept his promise to care for Lee's large family. They had spent the winter in tents while all the others were living in cabins.

Despite his anger Lee accepted new tasks assigned by Young. As Lee struggled to feed the poor and prepare for the difficult migration to Salt Lake City, he became disgusted with the lazy and jealous people in the Mormon community and longed for his heavenly reward. After hardship and much bickering during an extended stay in Iowa, only five of Lee's wives made the 125-day migration to Utah. The others went back to their parents or married other men.

Lee was not able to enjoy living in the promised land of Salt Lake City for more than a couple of years because Brigham Young asked him to play a leading role in the colonization of southern Utah. Though Lee had not yet even put a roof on his new house in Salt Lake City, he headed south with his wives and children. Again, he built up substantial property and remained available to undertake whatever the church required of him.

In his confession, Lee put blame for the Mountain Meadows Massacre on church and militia leaders in Cedar City. "At the time of the massacre, I and those with me, acted by virtue of positive orders from Isaac C. Haight and his associates at Cedar City," Lee wrote. "Before I started on my mission to the Mountain Meadows, I was told by Isaac C. Haight that his orders to me were the result of full consultation with Colonel William H. Dame and all in authority." Haight was the mayor of Cedar City, in charge of several local congregations and a battalion commander in the Mormon militia. Dame was the senior commander for the militia in southern Utah. Lee told about a night-long meeting with Haight in which the church leader recounted many stories about anti-Mormon sentiments of the people in the Fancher wagon train. Haight told him that the emigrants had poisoned springs, ravished Mormon women along their route and that those who had killed Joseph Smith were members of the wagon train. When Lee asked who was ordering the attack, Haight responded that the direction was coming from "all in authority." Lee in his autobiography said that since he also talked to Apostle George A. Smith, he believed he was carrying out orders from Brigham Young.

After the massacre Lee made a personal report to Brigham Young and resumed his life as a local leader in the Mormon community. He attended the state Legislature in Salt Lake City as a representative of his county and met an English emigrant named Emma Batchelor, whom he took as his 17th wife.

Investigations of the massacre conducted by local officials exonerated themselves, though the second one mentioned Lee as being at the scene during the massacre. Lee went into hiding when a federal judge attempted to arrest those responsible. By using a spy glass, Lee was able to see his farm from a hideout in the mountains and return whenever it was safe. As a wide area around Mountain Meadows lost its population, the stake, or local church organization, was disbanded, removing the local officials, particularly Haight, from authority. Haight went into hiding in Arizona under an assumed name and died in exile. After Dame refused to accept any responsibility and told church officials he would name those responsible if any guilt was directed toward him, he was sent on a two-year mission to England. Over time, Lee gave up his offices, which included probate judge.

As the United States approached the Civil War, the focus on the massacre diminished. After Brigham Young passed through Mountain Meadows and incited his followers to tear down a monument to the victims which had been erected by the cavalry, he went to Lee's house, where he was lavishly entertained. Lee was soon named presiding elder of the church in his community.

Lee's luck changed when heavy rains washed away his mill and collapsed a mud brick home, killing two of his children. Neighbors began to talk about Lee's role in the massacre and his family began to be bullied. On another trip to southern Utah, Brigham Young slighted Lee, his adopted son, by sending him away from his personal procession. When dissidents within the Mormon Church began to criticize Young and a Utah newspaper faulted the Prophet for not punishing those responsible for the Mountain Meadows incident, Young ordered Lee to move to a more remote area. Though Lee followed those orders and moved to Kanab, Utah, to set up a sawmill, he was still excommunicated from the church.

Lee protested the excommunication to Brigham Young in person. "I asked him how it was that: I was held in fellowship 13 years for an act then committed and all of a sudden I must be cut off from this church," Lee wrote. "If it was wrong now, it certainly was wrong then. He replied that they had never learned the particulars until lately." Lee added that he had told the whole truth to Young shortly after the massacre. After Lee followed Young's suggestion that he tell the story to Apostle Erastus Snow, the apostle told him to return the next day. When Lee came back, Snow was not there, but had left a note. It told Lee not to try to implicate others "least you cause others to become accessory with you and thereby force them to inform upon you or to suffer. Our advice is, Trust no one. Make yourself scarce and keep out of the way."

In the early 1870s, when the federal government began to crack down on polygamy and placed more officers in Utah, Lee was not safe even in remote Kanab. So he was told to move down to the Colorado River crossing in Arizona, where he built Lee's Ferry. Though warrants had been issued for seven men, the sheriff decided to concentrate on Lee and arrest him during one of Lee's visits to southern Utah. He was found hiding in a straw stack near the home of one of his wives.

Lee had two trials. At his first trial, a witness testified that Lee was not at the meeting where it was decided to kill the emigrants. The defense focused on orders to kill that came down from militia leaders. The eight Mormon jury members voted for acquittal and the four non-Mormons voted to convict, resulting in a hung jury and mistrial.

After a stay of several months in prison and a brief release on bond, Lee went back to court for his second trial. The focus was completely different. There was little mention of orders from superiors. The prosecutors concentrated only on what Lee actually did. Witnesses said they could remember very little about what happened at the massacre, but all of them were adamant that Lee had killed a woman. Lee felt he was being made a scapegoat. The all-Mormon jury voted unanimously to convict.

When the governor offered to give Lee a pardon if he would name his accomplices, Lee refused. The condemned man was taken to the scene of the massacre to face a firing squad. Before he was shot, Lee proclaimed his innocence, confident of his place in eternity.

Lee's Ferry

Lee's Ferry – Drawing by Carol Sletten inspired by a John Hanson Beadle etching of the riverbank by Lee's Ferry - 1881

Lee's Ferry

While most rivers in the Southwest are small because of the limited local precipitation, the Colorado is huge, collecting the melting snows of the Colorado Rockies. In pioneer times, it carried a volume of water equal to a flow half a mile wide and 10 feet deep moving at the rate of one foot per second. It was a substantial barrier to north-south traffic between Utah and Arizona, especially because the river flowed through a very deep canyon. Even above the Grand Canyon, the cliffs along the river were nearly vertical and hundreds of feet high.

Early Spanish Conquistadors, American mountain men and Mormon missionaries crossed the Colorado using one of two fords known to natives. The "Crossing of the Fathers," now under Lake Powell, was somewhat the easier for mounted groups, but the Mormons focused on a spot 40 miles downstream just above the Grand Canyon as a better way to get settlers across with their wagons, livestock and goods.

As early as 1864, missionary Jacob Hamblin had crossed at the second location where the Colorado widens a bit as the Paria River joins from the north. The Mormons created a small military outpost they called Fort Meeks to protect settlers against hostile Navajos. The Paria River confluence was initially used as a ford when the Colorado River was low. But the wide canyon beneath the Vermillion Cliffs made the waters relatively calm and offered the possibility of operating a boat to ferry settlers across the river.

Several initial attempts to build boats and carry them to the site failed, but in 1864, Hamblin and his men were able to build a log raft at the Paria River confluence and move it back and forth across the Colorado.

It was in connection with explorer John Wesley Powell's 1870 visit to the Colorado River that the first boat was constructed at Lonely Dell, as the tiny village at the crossing was known. Powell sought assistance from Mormon leaders who assigned Hamblin and others to help. They hewed planks in Mormon settlements in Utah and carried them by horse and mule to the river, fashioning a boat 12 feet long and three feet wide. They called it the Canyon Maid.

To get a real ferry going, the Mormons needed someone who could get things done. They called on John D. Lee. He was an odd choice. As a leader of the Mormons and Indians who massacred a wagon train at Mountain Meadows, he was already ex-communicated from the church. Lee was hiding from U.S. government authorities while running a sawmill in Utah. Church leaders saw advantages to placing him in the remote isolated canyon. They probably didn't realize that choosing him would put his name on the map, and give him and his dark past a certain immortality. (The church realized its mistake too late, eventually sending their president to address a joint session of the Arizona Legislature to keep Lee's name off a bridge built at the site.)

Lee arrived with two of the six wives who remained from his 19 marriages, 13 of his children and a brother-in-law and his wife. They went to work on an engineering feat that today would start with an appropriation of tens of millions of dollars and an army of construction workers to build the boat, the supporting facilities and the access roads on both sides of the river. On Jan. 29, 1872, Lee's boat carried its first passengers, a band of 15 Navajos who had called to him from the opposite bank. Lee rowed the rickety Canyon Maid while Rachel, one of his wives, steered. This was less than two weeks after his wife Emma had given birth to a girl, Frances Dell, the first non-Native born at the site.

Lee quickly built a dam on a small creek to irrigate a field to provide food for the settlement. Lee divided his family, setting up a farm 25 miles from the crossing called The Pools for

Rachel and her children. Emma and her children stayed at Lonely Dell, which is how she described the ferryboat location by the river when she first saw it.

Lee lost many of his tools and the Canyon Maid when careless gold prospectors "borrowed" and lost them in their frenzied search for the yellow metal in the swift current. For a time, Lee had use of a boat left with him by explorer Powell. In fact, Emma served breakfast to Powell and his men after they made their famous run through the Grand Canyon. It was among the first of many meals she prepared for travelers at the site.

Lee soon crafted another skiff from local lumber. The first real ferryboat was knocked together in three days by a team of Mormon carpenters who arrived with a load of lumber from Utah. It was framed by two timbers 26 feet long and connected by two-inch thick boards that served as the bottom and another layer of boards that formed the deck. The craft, eight and a half feet wide, could carry one wagon and team across the river. It was propelled by oars.

A construction team of 25 men arrived to build a winding road up from the river on the south side. High water quickly washed away the ferryboat and a new more crude vessel was fashioned.

Two years after Lee first arrived at the river crossing, he was arrested and put on trial. His wife Emma remained at the location and continued to own the ferry. She operated it with the help of her children and often a hired ferryman. Getting the big boat across the river in high water was difficult. The current would carry it far down stream each time it was rowed across so it had to be towed back upstream after each trip. It eventually capsized during a crossing. Many were saved, but the accident took the life of Bishop Lorenzo Roundy.

After Lee was executed, Mormon interests began bar-

73

gaining to buy the site of the ferry from Emma. She finally settled for a small amount of cash and a promise of livestock.

After Emma left in 1879, a new ferryboat was constructed. It was 47 feet in length and 13 $^1/_2$ feet wide. The large craft could only be used during the nine months of the year when the river was low. A small skiff was used during high water. In 1899, an overhead steel cable was used to keep a new ferry from going too far down river during its crossings.

Adolpha Johnson, the last ferryman, died in the last ferryboat when it went down in 1928. Only weeks later, a bridge was completed over the Colorado River at the site, making the ferry unnecessary after 55 years of operation.

Today, Lee's Ferry and Lonely Dell Ranch are a Historic District within the Glen Canyon National Recreation Area. The gorgeous scenery and excellent trout fishing bring thousands of visitors to the well-preserved 19th century buildings and irrigation works that sustained the tiny community. They can see pear, apricot, peach and plum trees growing at the site, a tribute to Emma Lee's orchard planted nearly 150 years ago.

Minnie Guenther

Drawing by Carol Sletten based on a photograph of Minnie with one of her nine children.

Minnie Guenther's Move To Her Missionary Field

Minnie was born in Neilsville, Wisconsin (1) and spent her life working on the White Mountain Apache Reservation (2)

Minnie (Knoop) Guenther Timeline

1890 Born in Neilsville, Wisconsin.

1910 Marrried to E. Edgar Guenther.

1910 Began missionary work on the White Mountain
Apache Reservation, opened a school.

1912 Meterorites hit wide area of reservation.

1913 Daughter Winonah born.

1914 Rode out into the countryside on a horse to treat
Apaches during a whooping cough epidemic.

1914 Government discontinued rations for Apaches.

1914 Son Edgar T. born.

1915 Major earthquake struck reservation.

1916 Son E. Roland born.

1916 Heavy snow and rain flood farms, wickiups, houses
and wash away bridges.

1918 Daughter Winifred born.

1918 Roman Catholics made major missionary push on
reservation.

1918-19 Great flu epidemic.

1921 Daughter Dorothea born.

1922 Chief Alchesay along with 100 members of his tribe
baptized during dedication ceremony for new church in
Whiteriver.

1922 Fort Apache abandoned by army.

1923 Opened orphanage in Whiteriver.

1923 Son Arthur Alchesay born.

1927 Daughter Ruth born.

1929 Another whooping cough epidemic struck reservation.

1933 Son Jonathan born.

1933 Meningitis epidemic.

1935 Daughter Myrna born.

1940 Appointed Postmaster.

1961 Widowed.

1966 Arizona Mother of the Year.

1967 National Mother of the Year.

1982 Died on the White Mountain Apache Reservation.

1986 Inducted into the Arizona Women's Hall of Fame.

Lutherans

Martin Luther was a 16th century German monk who preached against corruption and abuses within the Catholic Church. His teachings were accepted by German leaders who sought independence from Rome, leading to the Thirty Years War. Luther was one of the main leaders of what became known as the Reformation.

As the church split north and south, Lutheranism became the state religion of much of northern Europe, particularly in parts of Germany and Scandinavia. Politics overrode the doctrinal differences between Luther and the Catholic theologians. Luther believed that people obtained heaven by faith in God, even though God knew in advance who would believe. Baptism was extremely important to Luther, who believed that heaven would be closed to anyone who had not received the rite.

When Lutheranism made the jump to America, it followed largely national lines, with church services held in the native languages of emigrants. Church organization also followed geographic lines with "Synods" established in each state. The Wisconsin Synod, largely made up of German emigrants, formed the most conservative end of the spectrum while most other groups began merging into a common denomination closely aligned with other protestant churches.

The Wisconsin Lutherans take a very strict view on their doctrine of predestination and refuse to pray with any other denominations, even other Lutherans, if their doctrine differs even slightly.

Rev. E. Edgar Guenther

Drawing by Carol Sletten based on a photograph

Rev. E. Edgar Guenther

For some seminary graduates, the prospect of a life of poverty and hard work on a remote Indian reservation in Arizona would have evoked trepidation and fear of the unknown. For Edgar Guenther, who grew up in South Dakota gathering buffalo manure to burn for heat in the bitter winters and skinning gophers to earn money, coping with crushing adversity was just the expected undertaking of each and every day.

Guenther, born in 1885, was the son of German emigrants who had a South Dakota homestead and little other than "a horse with the heaves and a kitchen table with crooked legs." He was a promising student in grade school and was selected to attend Dr. Martin Luther College in New Ulm, as well as a Lutheran seminary.

When a letter was read asking for one of the graduates to serve as a missionary to the Apache Indians, he rushed to accept, and quickly married Minnie Knoop since he was advised not to go alone. They first stopped in Globe, Arizona, to learn from a missionary to the San Carlos Apache. The older man sent them on to the White Mountain reservation with these words of advice. "Ask for nothing. Promise nothing," because he said that the mission board would recall Guenther if he asked them for help, and the Indians would not trust him if he disappointed.

Though the White Mountain Apache Reservation was only across the Black River from the San Carlos Reservation, the Guenthers' journey to their new home was nearly 800 miles. They had to go from Globe to Deming, N.M., and then to Albuquerque before turning west again and going to Holbrook. "After 30 miles of travel and a night under the stars with the bugs at Snowflake and a second night 30 miles later in a freezing cold 'hotel' in Showlow, on the third night they finally arrived in Whiteriver, the headquarters for the whole reservation," according to a biography published by the church. After the superintendent of the reservation failed in his efforts to discourage them, the newlyweds went on to settle into their tiny house in East Fork.

At first, they worked mainly by making camp calls, riding out to visit the Apaches where they lived. "After arriving and chatting for a while, he would find suitable place for the service," the biography says. "Minnie would set up a portable organ and begin playing. After a hymn there would be a sermon and prayers. He would give them some literature and then move on."

They built a school and attracted students by serving meals, which they paid for themselves. Minnie did the cooking in her own kitchen while Edgar borrowed horses and a wagon to collect scrap lumber to make desks. Since there were no books, they bought a typewriter and made their own.

Guenther wanted to approach Alchesay, the famous chief of the White Mountain Apaches who had served as a scout to General Crook during the Apache wars, but he knew he needed to wait until the time was right. "One day when Guenther was out by himself looking for the sick to minister to, he found Alchesay sick with the flu," the biography says. "He provided him with some bedding, medicine and had a short devotion." After that Alchesay became friends with Ivnashood Ndaezn (the tall missionary) and brought his tribe to Guenther's church to be baptized.

In those times, many Apache infants were killed, especially if they had deformities. "One day for example he was called to an Apache camp two miles away," the Guenther biography says. "There was a debate going on about what to do with a baby born with six fingers on each hand. The grandmother said they should kill it now. Guenther instantly grabbed a knife, ran it through the flames and cut off one of his fingers on each hand. The baby's life was saved."

If twins were born, one of them was often killed because it was believed that a double birth was the result of immorality. There were also many children whose parents died in epidemics, which were constantly sweeping through the reservation. The Guenthers created an orphanage to save those children.

The reverend suffered a heart attack when he was building a church in 1945, and began to slow down a little bit when his son Arthur Alchesay Guenther became his assistant pastor. Though Edgar lived in Tucson during his final years because the lower elevation made it easier for him to breathe, he returned to Whiteriver one last time in 1961 to celebrate his 75th birthday and the 50th anniversary of his work among the Apaches. More than 1,500 people gathered to mark the occasion and honor the tall missionary. He died in Tucson two months later and was buried in the Whiteriver cemetery.

Chief Alchesay "A-1"

Detail of a drawing by Carol Sletten based on a photograph of Alchesay with Gen. George Crook.

Apache Reservations

The two Apache reservations of east-central Arizona were established by President Ulysses Grant in 1871 in response to the massacre of friendly Indians at Fort Grant in southern Arizona.

The two reserves, which had a total land area the size of Connecticut, were intended to create a place where Apaches could be safe from conflicts with settlers, while allowing whites the peaceful use of the rest of Arizona. For bands that already lived on the land of the new reservations, it was relatively good news. But for Apaches who were forced to move to the reservation from their territories in other Southwest locations, it was a concentration camp. This was especially so when the government wanted all the Indians to live on inhospitable and unhealthy areas around San Carlos. The Chiricahua from southern Arizona and the Warm Springs Apaches from New Mexico were most resistant to the resettlement.

Fort Apache, at the confluence of two branches of the White River, had been established a year earlier in the heart of the country that would become the northern reservation. The name "Fort Apache" has traveled around the world as a symbol of an isolated stronghold surrounded by active hostiles. But the real Fort Apache never had a stockade and was rarely attacked. It served more as a government administration center, a distribution point for rations, a jail and a cavalry base for offensive operations against hostiles.

Lozen

Drawing by Carol Sletten

Journey of a Warrior Woman

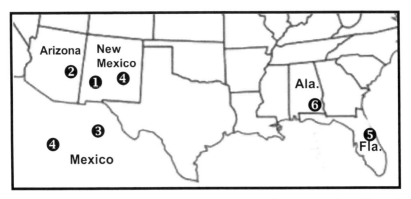

Lozen was born in the Warm Springs area of New Mexico (1) and taken with her tribe to the San Carlos Reservation in Arizona (2). When her brother, Chief Victorio, was killed in Mexico at Tres Castillos (3) she raided (4) throughout Arizona, New Mexico and Mexico with Chief Nana and Geronimo. After the Apaches surrendered, they were taken to Fort Marion, Florida (5). She died in a prisoner of war camp in Alabama (6).

Lozen Timeline

1840 Born in the Warm Springs area of New Mexico.

1848 U.S. fought war with Mexico, gaining claim to much of the Southwest.

1853 U.S. purchased portion of Arizona and New Mexico south of Gila River.

1861 Civil War began, leading to the withdrawal of troops from Arizona and New Mexico.

1862 Troops from North and South both re-entered Southwest, renewing conflict with Apaches.

1863 Apache chief Mangas Coloradas murdered by whites, Lozen's brother Victorio becomes chief.

1877 Chiricahua Apaches removed to desolate reservation at San Carlos, Arizona.

1879 Victorio left San Carlos reservation for the last time, beginning "Victorio's War" and terrorizing settlements in New Mexico and Mexico. Lozen used her skills for sensing the presence of the enemy, stealing horses and traveling unseen to protect Victorio's band.

1880 Lozen left the band to care for a woman in childbirth.

1880 Victorio killed by Mexican troops at Tres Castillos south of El Paso.

1881 Lozen helped to steal ammunition from soldiers at the Battle of Cibecue, leading a mule with crates of bullets strapped to its pack saddle. She headed to Mexico along with Chief Nana. They raided in Arizona and New Mexico, exacting revenge for the killing of

Victorio.

1886 Lozen and Nana, who had joined forces with Geronimo, surrendered to U.S. forces in Mexico.

1886 Taken as a prisoner of war to Florida.

1890 Died at a prisoner of war camp in Alabama.

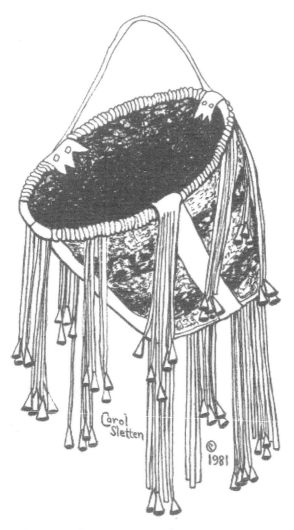

Apache Burden Basket

Drawing by Carol Sletten

Apaches

Apaches were among the last of the Native Americans to come to the New World. Though it is believed that they crossed over from Asia 10,000 years ago, they didn't make it to Arizona until about 1,000 years ago. They were hunter-gatherers and experts at living in the Southwest mountain environment.

Before coming to the Southwest, they harvested only wild plants, but after contact with the Pueblo people they became farmers.

In the high elevations, corn was planted as early as April so it would mature before the fall frosts, but in lower elevations planting continued into July. Water was channeled onto tiny fields from streams or springs.

Apaches moved seasonally to take advantage of the plants that each area offered. They made different kinds of shelters in these varied environments. For one type of gowa or wickiup, they tied poles together at one end and spread out the opposite end to create a pointed structure which they covered with brush. In the domed gowa, a pole would stretch from the ground, to the top and then back to the ground on the other side. For more temporary residences, they would place rocks in a ring to serve as a windbreak.

Early Apaches used bows and arrows, spears, throwing sticks, hooked sticks and clubs. White Mountain Apaches wrapped their bows in sinew to add strength and made bowstrings from sinew or rawhide. An Apache arrow was made by placing a wooden foreshaft onto a reed. They also had one-piece wooden arrows.

Apaches used deerskin for clothing. The hide was soaked in water, scraped with a bone to remove the hair, meat and fat, and then soaked again. The brains of the deer were applied to soften the leather before additional soaking.

In addition to deer and antelope, they hunted rabbits and other small animals, but because of taboos they rarely ate bear or fish.

Apaches used baskets ingeniously for many domestic purposes. Their light weight made them compatible with the people's mobile lifestyle. Mulberry baskets were especially useful because the dense wood was durable enough, when moist, to be used in cooking.

Cradleboards were used to restrain and carry infants. They were made from a wooden hoop covered with strips of yucca or other plants. The inside was padded with soft moss and a woven canopy protected the child's head from the sun.

Apaches made music with gourd rattles, wooden flutes and buckskin-covered drums, which were beaten with their hands or hooped sticks. Violins were made from hollow pieces of walnut or agave stalks. They were strung with a single piece of sinew and played with a horsehair bow.

Many games were played, some with buckskin playing cards, wooden dice or handmade darts. One of the longest contests involved guessing which of four shoes contained a bone. It was played all night until the score reached 104 to nothing.

Apache Wars

Apaches fought the European invasion of what is now Arizona for 346 years, from the time of Coronado's trip across Arizona in 1540 until Geronimo finally surrendered in 1886. The reason that conflict was one of the longest in history can be attributed to the desolate nature of the Arizona landscape and how skillful the Apaches were in defending their homeland.

Since Coronado found no riches in Arizona, the Spanish never considered it worthwhile to pay for the type of military campaign that would have been necessary to conquer the remote northern frontier of their New World empire. By the late 1500s, the Spanish were settling among the Pimas and other tribes in what is now southern Arizona, but they made little progress in moving civilization north, despite centuries of effort.

Though the Spanish established forts in what is now northern Mexico, they were not much of a barrier to Apache raiders who slipped easily between them. For a time, the Spanish adopted a policy of feeding the Apaches and giving them liquor, which kept them off the warpath. The government soon ran out of money and abandoned the policy. At other times, the Spanish and Mexican governments paid a bounty for Apache scalps, hoping to exterminate their enemies.

Much of northern Arizona was left to the Apaches until the Southwest came under American control with the Mexican War in 1848. The Civil War caused the U.S. military to withdraw from the area without subduing the Apaches. After the conflict, rich mineral discoveries near Wickenburg, Prescott, Globe and areas in southern Arizona brought an influx of white settlers who called on the military for protection.

The Apaches, who had formerly been able to roam freely over most of the state and into Mexico, were concentrated in the east-central mountains, which, fortunately for them, were largely without mineral wealth. The relocation of Apaches from other areas into east-central Arizona resulted in the battles of the later Apache Wars, the last major conflicts with native peoples in the United States.

Nana

Adapted from an 1887 illustration in Century magazine

Nana

Nana, born when the United States was less than 25 years old, survived to be a leader in the last Indian War and was actively fighting the cavalry as a guerrilla leader and horse soldier into his 80s.

Though he didn't start life among the highest ranking member of his tribe, he survived many decades of combat to become a noted war chief.

Kas-tziden, or broken foot, was born among the Warm Springs Apache in New Mexico around 1800 when the United States was still confined to the east bank of the Mississippi River. The warrior became known by the Spanish "Nana," or grandma, only later in life. He married Geronimo's sister, the daughter of a chief named Mahko, and fought with Mangas Coloradas, or Red Sleeves, against the American occupation of New Mexico.

Nana served under the successors to the treacherously slain Mangas Coloradas, including Chiefs Cochise, Taza and Victorio. When Victorio was killed in Mexico, Nana joined the slain chief's sister, Lozen, to lead one of the last active campaigns against white rule. With as few as 15 warriors, Nana, in his 80s, fought the cavalry, eluding 1,400 soldiers on a 1,000-mile journey of destruction across the Southwest. He united his forces with Geronimo and continued the struggle until 1886. He was taken with the other hostiles to Florida and died in Oklahoma in 1896.

Victorio

Drawing by Carol Sletten

Victorio

Victorio, born in what is now New Mexico in about 1820, was the son and grandson of leading men within his tribe. Though the names of his parents are not known, stories that he was a Mexican captive are certainly false. He was a very promising young man, named, along with his cousin Loco, as band leader after their chief was killed. They were also chosen by Mangas Coloradas to lead the entire Warm Springs Apache Tribe upon his death.

When Americans took over administration of New Mexico after the Mexican War, Victorio signed a treaty. He pledged to settle down on land in New Mexico in exchange for peace with the whites and trade goods. The army was supposed to protect the Apaches from scalp hunters, who were still collecting bounties from the Mexican government for slain Apaches. But when sufficient rations were not provided, the Apaches raided Mexico.

After the Civil War broke out and soldiers left New Mexico to join the conflict, the Apaches thought they had chased the Americans out. But the soldiers soon returned in the uniforms of their contending armies, the South from Texas and the North from California. Both sides were hostile to the Apaches.

When Mangas Coloradas went to the mining town of Piños Altos, hoping to negotiate peace, he was arrested, bound, tortured with hot irons and eventually shot. His head was cut off, boiled and sent to a museum in the East.

Victorio was horrified. "The murder, he thought, was barbaric, but the mutilation of the remains was an act that far exceeded even that," Victorio's biography says. Apaches believed that the mutilation would affect their leader in the afterlife. Victorio became the main leader of the Chiricahua. After a long stalemate, he moved his tribe to a new reservation in the Tularosa Valley of New Mexico, about one hundred miles from their traditional homes.

Though Victorio's people were briefly allowed to return to their homes, the army and Indian police eventually arrived to take them to the hot and desolate San Carlos, Arizona, where they faced hunger, sickness and death. Smallpox broke out even when they were on the trail to the inhospitable reservation. Victorio, after deciding that the Apaches were being kept at San Carlos to die, broke out, leading more than 300 people in an escape from the reservation. They went north to the Navajo Reservation and surrendered there at Fort Wingate, eventually being allowed to return to their home in New Mexico. But that was only temporary.

When soldiers again came to take Victorio and his people to San Carlos, they escaped to Old Mexico. Victorio went to the Mescalero Reservation in eastern New Mexico, but left when he was refused food. His anger increased when the army attacked people he had left behind in the Warm Springs area, especially since the soldiers killed women and children. Victorio would draw the cavalry into a canyon and attack from the high ground, often capturing horses, mules and supplies as the soldiers were forced to retreat. After he finally abandoned his Warm Springs homeland, Victorio went to Mexico. A spy that he sent into a village learned that the people were plotting to trap and kill Victorio so the chief lured the villagers into ambushes and killed many of their men before heading back to the United States and the sacred Warm Springs. As the war dragged on, Victorio's camp was surrounded and attacked by the Americans, causing the loss of many warriors. They again fled to Mexico.

Pursued by Mexican and American troops, Victorio's band camped at the foot of three small mountains, Tres Castillos. They were attacked after dark by hundreds of

Mexican troops and Indian allies from other tribes. Initially, Victorio tried to retreat into the higher ground of the small mountains. The Apaches sang their death songs as both sides waited for daylight. When the Mexicans attacked at dawn, the warriors held them off for two hours until their ammunition ran out. Then the Mexicans advanced and killed the survivors, missing only the few women and children who had managed to slip away during the night. Some reports say that Victorio, wounded multiple times, took his own life with a knife.

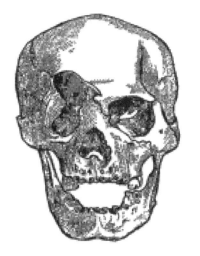 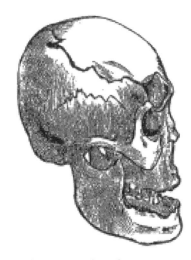

From a 19th century drawing

Skull of Mangas Coloradas

The day after Mangas Coloradas (Red Sleeves) was murdered, U.S. soldiers cut off his head, boiled it and sent
the skull to Orson Squire Fowler, a phrenologist in New
York City. It was displayed at Fowler's Phrenological
Cabinet in New York. Apache tradition says the skull
was displayed at the Smithsonian Institution, but the Institution has no record of the skull.

Apache Religion

In traditional Apache belief, all things, both animate and inanimate, have a spirit or life force. Ussen, the Giver or Life, is the source of all Power. Apache religion has been passed down from generation to generation through a group of traditional tales that are told only during the cold months of winter.

Many of the stories focus on a family of Apache deities: White Changing Woman, the twins, Born for Water and Killer of Enemies, and the boys' fathers, Sun and Water Old Man. Changing Woman is also called White Painted Woman and White Shell Woman. In the stories, the twins go on a journey to save the world from monsters.

Spider Woman, the trickster Coyote, and the Mountain Spirits or Gans are also sacred characters. Crown Dancers represent the Gans in ceremonies. The four Gans, symbolizing the four directions, and a clown who appears with them, have a special role in teaching the people how to live in righteousness.

Individuals can obtain a supernatural Power to aid them in healing, hunting, battle or other activities through dreams and visions. Ghosts, the spirits of the dead, are the source of dread, and witches, who have obtained Power for evil, are feared.

Medicine men are paid to perform curing ceremonies. They use traditional chants, drumbeats, herbs and sacred objects to help them make spiritual connections. Today the Sunrise Ceremony, in which a girl's passage into womanhood is marked by a multi-day ceremony, is one of the strongest ties to tradition for modern Apaches.

Times of severe stress, when old faiths seem ineffective and people look for help beyond the current circumstances, often produce new religious beliefs. The Apaches of east-central Arizona had four cults. The first was started by

102

Noche'Del'Klinne in 1881 and resulted in the Cibecue Uprising. The second was led by Das Lan, another Cibecue
prophet. It ended when the medicine man had followers cut
off his head and he didn't rise again after three days as he had
promised. The third movement was led by a prophet known
by his government tag number of P-1, and his son P-6. It
fizzled out after predictions about the world ending didn't come
true. Silas John Edwards, known as the Apache Jesus, created the fourth religious movement. He combined elements of
Christianity, traditional Apache beliefs and a snake dance in
his ceremonies. His influence diminished when he was convicted of murdering his wife.

Cibecue Uprising

Though Emma Lee and Lozen didn't know each other, their lives were both affected by the Cibecue Uprising in 1881.

The Ghost Dance movement which was sweeping through Indian Country during that time was not a traditional Native religion. It was more of a cult led by charismatic men who claimed to have supernatural power that would restore the Indian way of life.

Noche'Del'Klinne, a former Apache Scout and medicine man, became the leader of one of these movements. He held dances in the village of Cibecue where he promised to raise Apache chiefs from the dead and drive whites from Apache land. Some accounts say Victorio was one of the chiefs to be raised.

Government officials were worried that the dances would rile up the Indians and send them on the warpath. They sent word for the medicine man to make the 40-mile trip to Fort Apache. But when he made the long trek on foot, they ignored him so he returned to Cibecue to resume his dances.

Some accounts say Geronimo and Nana saw Victorio and other Apache chiefs begin to rise from the dead.

When soldiers came to stop the dances, Noche'Del'Klinne was killed and fighting broke out. Apache Scouts defected to fight on the side of the worshippers against the soldiers. The captain of the cavalry was killed and a number of soldiers were wounded.

Lozen, who witnessed the killing of the medicine man, decided to use her horse power to steal an army mule loaded with ammunition boxes. She lay low across her horse to avoid the whizzing bullets and led the mule away with the precious ammunition.

The soldiers retreated to Fort Apache and hunkered down as shots were fired into the buildings. The Cibecue Apaches broke from the reservation and headed northwest, killing several settlers before they were overtaken and defeated in the battle of Chevlon Canyon. Geronimo soon headed back to Mexico, and Nana and Lozen followed.

At that time Emma was living with her new husband, Frank French, in Forestdale, a contested valley that Mormons were claiming on the Apache Reservation. The violence of the Cibecue Uprising convinced the settlers to give up on the valley and move north off the reservation.

Three Apache Scouts were convicted of fighting against the cavalry and hanged. A number of Apaches who are prominent on the reservation today are descendants of Scouts who switched sides when the medicine man was killed.

Geronimo

Drawing by Carol Sletten

106

Geronimo

While many Apache leaders were great statesmen earnestly seeking a solution that would allow their people to live in peace, Geronimo loved the warpath.

He was born about 1829 into the Bedonkohe sub-tribe of the Chiricahua Apache in an area near the present New Mexico-Arizona state line just southeast of Arizona's White Mountains.

He told a tale about his wife, mother and children being killed by Mexican soldiers when he was a child, but historians discount the account, believing Geronimo at least partially manufactured the tale when he was attempting to get sympathy for his situation as prisoner of war.

A medicine man, Geronimo became a war leader. He served under Naiche, the son of Cochise who became chief of the Chiricahua when Cochise died. After one of his surrenders, Geronimo and his people were placed at Turkey Creek, just east of Fort Apache on the White Mountain Apache reservation.

Whenever Geronimo was on the reservation, he was plotting his next breakout and caching food and weapons to retrieve on his flight to Mexico.

Some insight into Geronimo's world view is expressed in the dialogue from one of his many peace talks, reported by scout Tom Horn. "I listened to your talk yesterday and it made me feel that I had done some great wrong," Geronimo said. "Perhaps I have done wrong, as a white man looks at my actions. I know that a white man does not see as an Apache sees, and I know that what is life to a white man is death to an Apache. ... You complain of my people raiding and killing up in the Americans' country. Do you not think I should complain of your war chief killing my warriors? Well, I make no complaint of that kind, for so, and in that fashion, do many of my young men want to die. I know, and my men know, that sooner or later all will get killed who keep up such a life."

In this instance, and many others, Geronimo chose to make peace when there was no opportunity to make war. On his final surrender, the government was well past patience, taking the old warrior and his men by train to Florida as prisoners of war. He died on an Oklahoma reservation in 1909 after hard drinking caused him to fall from his horse.

By staying at war with the United States and Mexico after other leaders had surrendered or been killed, Geronimo became the most famous Native American of all time.

Imprisonment

(From *Story of the American West*)

The government had to decide what to do with the Apaches who surrendered in 1886. Some suggested shipping them to Florida to make sure they could never escape and return to Arizona and Mexico. The *St. Johns Herald* wanted a final solution. "Don't ship rattlesnakes to Florida. ... Kill 'em."

The black "Buffalo Soldiers" of the 10th Cavalry were in charge of loading the prisoners onto wagons and taking them to the railroad in Holbrook. The hostiles were taken in the first two trips, but the government had plans to include other passengers on the third trip.

Geronimo's biographer, E.M Halliday, wrote: "Four hundred Chiricahuas at Fort Apache, who had remained loyal all through Geronimo's last rampage, were summarily rounded up and sent off to Fort Marion (Florida) also. Not exempted were many Apache Scouts who had served [General George] Crook with absolute fidelity, and to the end of his days the General never lost his smoldering indignation at this treatment."

"We didn't know where we were to be taken from Holbrook," Samuel Kenoi, was quoted as saying in *Geronimo and the End of the Indian Wars* by C.L. Sonnichsen. "Some thought we were going to be taken to the ocean and thrown in. Some thought we were going to be killed in some other way."

"It was the first time most of us had seen a train," said Kenoi. "When the train was coming along the river and it whistled, many said it was run by lightning, and they began to pray to the train."

Children ran away, but the train was eventually loaded.

"Left behind as the train slowly rolled along were the tribe's livestock, dogs, and several piles of belongings that could not be fitted into the two baggage cars," according to an Apache account of the scene in *Survival of the Spirit* by H. Henrietta Stockel. "The personal belongings were quickly picked over by souvenir hunters. The horses were rounded up by the soldiers and later sold at auction at Fort Union, New Mexico. The camp dogs, which had faithfully followed the tribe from Fort Apache, were distraught at being separated from their masters and ran pitifully, howling and yapping, beside the train. Some kept up for almost 20 miles."

The men were placed at Fort Pickens in Florida while their families were kept at Fort Marion, 200 miles away.

The *St. Johns Herald* reported that the president had concluded that military tribunals did not have authority to try the captives and that they could not get a fair trial by civilian courts in the territories. So, he opted for life imprisonment without trial. "As a matter of fact the transfer of the savages to Florida, means a lingering death and experienced army officers do not think there will be one of them alive at the end of five years," the newspaper wrote. It later added, "Geronimo and his band are said to be surrendering to the climate of Florida at the rate of four a day. There are 454 bucks, squaws and papooses at Fort Marion, while Geronimo and twelve or fifteen others are at Fort Pickens."

General George Crook, however, did not give up on the Apaches. From his new post in Omaha, he lobbied to have them moved to Oklahoma, arranging for the transfer before he died in 1890. The tribe, descended from the original 81 captives who came from Florida, now numbers nearly 700, with 300 of them living in Oklahoma.

Acknowledgements

I'm very grateful to my husband, Eric Kramer, and to all the people who helped and encouraged me while I was writing *Three Strong Western Women*, especially to Karen Alderson, Melissa Colelay Bonney, Barb Davis, Sheryl Eaton, Julie Holtan, Marty and Ron LaMar, Barbara Lashmet, Penny Albright Peterson and A.J. Taylor.

Selected Bibliography

Apache Indian Baskets, by Clara Lee Tanner, University of
Arizona Press, Tucson, Arizona, 1982

*Apache Reservation, Indigenous Peoples & the American
State*, by Richard J. Perry, University of Texas Press,
Austin, Texas, 1993

Arizona Women's Hall of Fame, Minnie Knoop Guenther,
Arizona State Library, Phoenix, Arizona, 1986

*Blood of the Prophets: Brigham Young and the Massacre
at Mountain Meadows* by Will Bagley, University of
Oklahoma Press, Norman, Oklahoma, 2004

*Devil's Gate, Brigham Young and the Great Mormon
Handcart Tragedy*, by David Roberts, Simon &
Schuster, New York, 2008

*Don't Let the Sun Step Over You, A White Mountain
Apache Family Life, 1860-1975*, by Eva Tulene Watt
with assistance from Keith H. Basso, University of Arizona Press, 2004

E. Edgar Guenther, the Lord's Faithful Servant, a document
published by the Wisconsin Evangelical Lutheran Synod.

Emma Lee, by Juanita Brooks, Utah State University Press,
Logan, Utah, 1978

The Ghost Dance, by James Mooney, JG Press, Dighton,
Massachusetts. 1996

Guenther Family History, Oral Histories of Pinetop, Lakeside,
McNary, Whiteriver, Arizona State Library, Phoenix, Arizona 1977

The Image of Arizona, Pictures from the Past, by Andrew
Wallace, University of New Mexico Press, 1971

*In the Days of Victorio, Recollections of a Warm Springs
Apache,* by Eve Ball, University of Arizona Press, Tucson, Arizona, 1970

Indeh, An Apache Odyssey, by Eve Ball, University of Oklahoma Press, Norman, Oklahoma 1980

John Doyle Lee, Zealot, Pioneer Builder, Scapegoat, by
Juanita Brooks, Utah State University Press, Logan,
Utah, 1992

Lee's Ferry, From Mormon Crossing to National Park,

by P.T. Reilly, Utah State University Press, Logan, Utah, 1997

Mormonism Unveiled, The Life and Confession of John D. Lee and Complete Life of Brigham Young, by John D. Lee, University of New Mexico Press, Albuquerque, 2008

The Mountain Meadows Massacre, by Juanita Brooks, University of Oklahoma Press, Norman, Oklahoma, 2012

The People Called Apache, by Thomas E. Mails, BDD Illustrated Books, New York, 1974

Reaping the Whirlwind, the Apache Wars, by Peter Aleshire, Facts on File, New York, 1998

Story of the American West, Legends of Arizona, by Carol Sletten & Eric Kramer, Wolf Water Press, Pinetop, Arizona, 2011

Survival of the Spirit, Chiricahua Apaches in Captivity, by Henrietta Stockel, University of Nevada Press, Reno, Nevada, 1995

Territorial Women's Memorial Rose Garden, Sharlot Hall Museum, Prescott, Arizona, 1997

Victorio: Apache Warrior and Chief, by Kathleen P. Chamberlain, University of Oklahoma Press, Norman, Oklahoma, 2012

Warrior Woman, The Story of Lozen, Apache Warrior and Shaman, by Peter Aleshire, St. Martin's Press, New York, 2001

Western Apache Heritage, People of the Mountain Corridor, by Richard J. Perry, University of Texas Press, Austin, Texas, 1991

The Western Apache, Living With the Land Before 1950, by Winfred Buskirk, University of Oklahoma Press, Norman, Oklahoma, 1986

Western Apache Material Culture, The Goodwin and Guenther collections, Edited by Alan Ferg, The Arizona State Museum, Tucson, Arizona, 1987

Index

INDEX

More complete index at www.ThreeStrongWesternWomen.com

About the Authors

Carol Sletten is an illustrator and writer who has studied and continues to study Apache culture and the history of the West through scholarship, interviews, friendships and community projects.

Her husband, Eric Kramer, is a successful journalist who rose to supervisory and managerial positions at the Associated Press, United Press International and Dow Jones & Co. while maintaining ties to rural Arizona.

They live and work in a cabin a mile from the Fort Apache Reservation in Arizona's White Mountains.

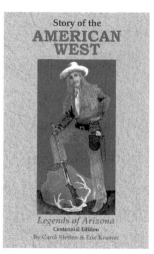

Carol's forthcoming project is a novel called *The Apache Jesus*, the story of a religious leader accused of murdering his wife after authorities began to fear his growing power.

Their Arizona Centennial Project was *Story of the American West, Legends of Arizona*. The book traces the pre-history and history of the White Mountains and surrounding area from the formation of the geology to the eve of World War II, recounting the lives of the Apaches, Mountain Men, Hispanics, Soldiers, Mormons, Cowboys, Blacks, Outlaws and others who struggled in one of the last untamed regions of the West.

www.OakHillStudio.com
www.StoryOfTheAmericanWest.com